My CRAZY Life

A BOOK FOR KEEPING YOUR LIFE ON TRACK

This crazy life belongs to:

____

Nerd Crow

Welcome to this crazy thing called LIFE

Let's face it – women are the busiest people on the planet.

Every woman I know is juggling *at least* two jobs — usually some combination of school, work, home or kids. Some women are juggling all four! Seriously, having a fulfilling life is *not* for the weak.

Studies have shown that when we take care of ourselves — when we live *well* — we're better able to take care of the other important people in our lives too. With that in mind, I created this *My Crazy Life* tracker to help build habits of self-awareness and self-love when it comes to your body and your life. And if you think you don't have time to write down all this stuff because you're, you know, **busy,** I hear you. That's why this *undated* 6-month journal was made.

There's 26 weeks' worth of tracking goodness in here. Every week you get 4 pages designed to track all your *Crazy Life* needs. Fill out the different parts on a daily basis (water consumption, hours slept, etc.) and by the end of the week you will have a comprehensive snapshot of your life, along with your weight and measurements. In addition, I've included a super cute page for keeping track of your periods, and a 6-month graph for visualizing your weight loss progress.

I hope you will enjoy this *My Crazy Life* tracker. I tried to make it both useful *and* fun to use, so dig out your colored pens, pencils, markers, and highlighters and make each page uniquely your own.

Remember, Queen — *you* were made for greatness, so go get it, and then rock on. ♥

How to Use This Tracker

Remember you can fill out as much, or as little, of your tracker as you like. Don't feel like it's not worth doing unless you have loads of time to spend on it. Tracking is supposed to be fun while at the same time giving you important, life-changing information. 🙂

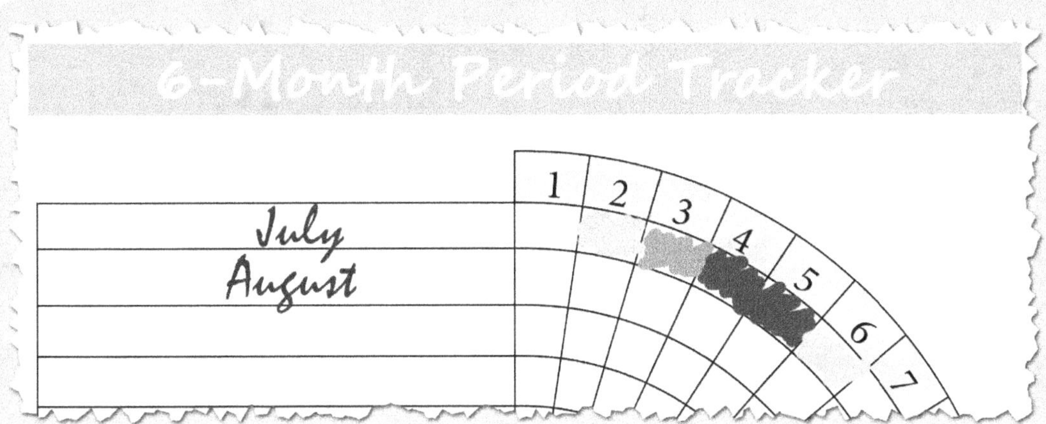

Fill in the boxes, or circles any way you like — color them in, check them off, X them out, *whatever*. Personally, I love to color them in. If you do that for the whole page, you've created a gorgeous mosaic that just happens to be useful. 🖤

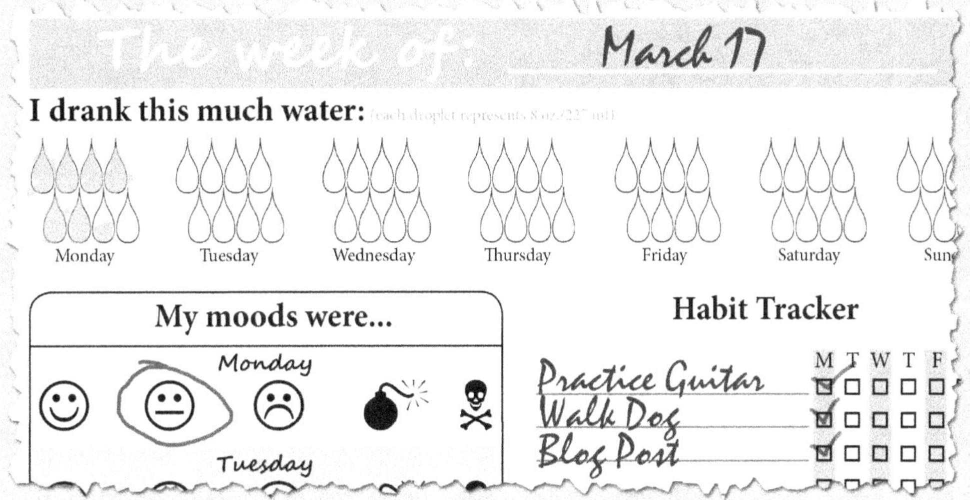

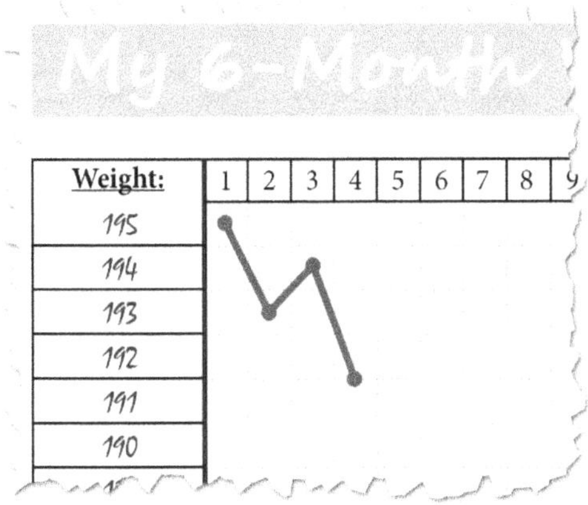

This is what I call my Instant Gratification Graph – fill it in every week as you go along, and by the end — *voilà* — you have a perfect snapshot of your weight loss victory.

Or defeat. 🙁

But what matters is that you tried, and it will be better next time (I promise) because then you will know so much more about yourself. 🖤

I drank this much water: (each droplet represents 8 oz./227 ml)

Monday   Tuesday   Wednesday   Thursday   Friday   Saturday   Sunday

My moods were...

Monday

Tuesday

Wednesday

Thursday

Friday

Saturday

Sunday

Habit Tracker

M T W T F S S

Inspirations ❀ Affirmations ❀ Gratitudes

Sleep Tracker ✿ Week of _______

Hours Slept

	M	T	W	T	F	S	S

12
11
10
9
8
7
6
5
4
3
2
1
0

Dreams

Stuff I did before bed...

Energy Level

E F M
E F T

E F W
E F T

E F F
E F S

E F S

Exercise Tracker

Type of Exercise	Amount	Notes	M	T	W	T	F	S	S
			☐	☐	☐	☐	☐	☐	☐
			☐	☐	☐	☐	☐	☐	☐
			☐	☐	☐	☐	☐	☐	☐
			☐	☐	☐	☐	☐	☐	☐
			☐	☐	☐	☐	☐	☐	☐
			☐	☐	☐	☐	☐	☐	☐
			☐	☐	☐	☐	☐	☐	☐
			☐	☐	☐	☐	☐	☐	☐
			☐	☐	☐	☐	☐	☐	☐
			☐	☐	☐	☐	☐	☐	☐

Food Tracker

Monday

Breakfast	
Lunch	
Dinner	
Snacks	

Tuesday

Breakfast	
Lunch	
Dinner	
Snacks	

Wednesday

Breakfast	
Lunch	
Dinner	
Snacks	

Thursday

Breakfast	
Lunch	
Dinner	
Snacks	

Friday

Breakfast	
Lunch	
Dinner	
Snacks	

Saturday

Breakfast	
Lunch	
Dinner	
Snacks	

Sunday

Breakfast	
Lunch	
Dinner	
Snacks	

Date: ____

Neck: ____

Chest: ____

Left Arm: ____

Right Arm: ____

Waist: ____

Hips: ____

Left Thigh: ____

Right Thigh: ____

Left Calf: ____

Right Calf: ____

Weekly Weigh-In

Weight: ____

I drank this much water: (each droplet represents 8 oz./227 ml)

Monday Tuesday Wednesday Thursday Friday Saturday Sunday

My moods were...

Monday

Tuesday

Wednesday

Thursday

Friday

Saturday

Sunday

Habit Tracker

M T W T F S S

Inspirations ❀ Affirmations ❀ Gratitudes

Sleep Tracker ❀ Week of _______

Hours Slept

M	T	W	T	F	S	S

12
11
10
9
8
7
6
5
4
3
2
1
0

Dreams

Stuff I did before bed...

Energy Level

E F
M

E F
T

E F
W

E F
T

E F
F

E F
S

E F
S

Exercise Tracker

Type of Exercise	Amount	Notes	M	T	W	T	F	S	S
			☐	☐	☐	☐	☐	☐	☐
			☐	☐	☐	☐	☐	☐	☐
			☐	☐	☐	☐	☐	☐	☐
			☐	☐	☐	☐	☐	☐	☐
			☐	☐	☐	☐	☐	☐	☐
			☐	☐	☐	☐	☐	☐	☐
			☐	☐	☐	☐	☐	☐	☐
			☐	☐	☐	☐	☐	☐	☐
			☐	☐	☐	☐	☐	☐	☐
			☐	☐	☐	☐	☐	☐	☐

Food Tracker

Monday

Breakfast	
Lunch	
Dinner	
Snacks	

Tuesday

Breakfast	
Lunch	
Dinner	
Snacks	

Wednesday

Breakfast	
Lunch	
Dinner	
Snacks	

Thursday

Breakfast	
Lunch	
Dinner	
Snacks	

Friday

Breakfast	
Lunch	
Dinner	
Snacks	

Saturday

Breakfast	
Lunch	
Dinner	
Snacks	

Sunday

Breakfast	
Lunch	
Dinner	
Snacks	

Date: _______________________________

Neck: _______________________________

Chest: _______________________________

Left Arm: _______________________________

Right Arm: _______________________________

Waist: _______________________________

Hips: _______________________________

Left Thigh: _______________________________

Right Thigh: _______________________________

Left Calf: _______________________________

Right Calf: _______________________________

Weekly Weigh-In

Weight: _______________________________

I drank this much water: (each droplet represents 8 oz./227 ml)

Monday | Tuesday | Wednesday | Thursday | Friday | Saturday | Sunday

My moods were...

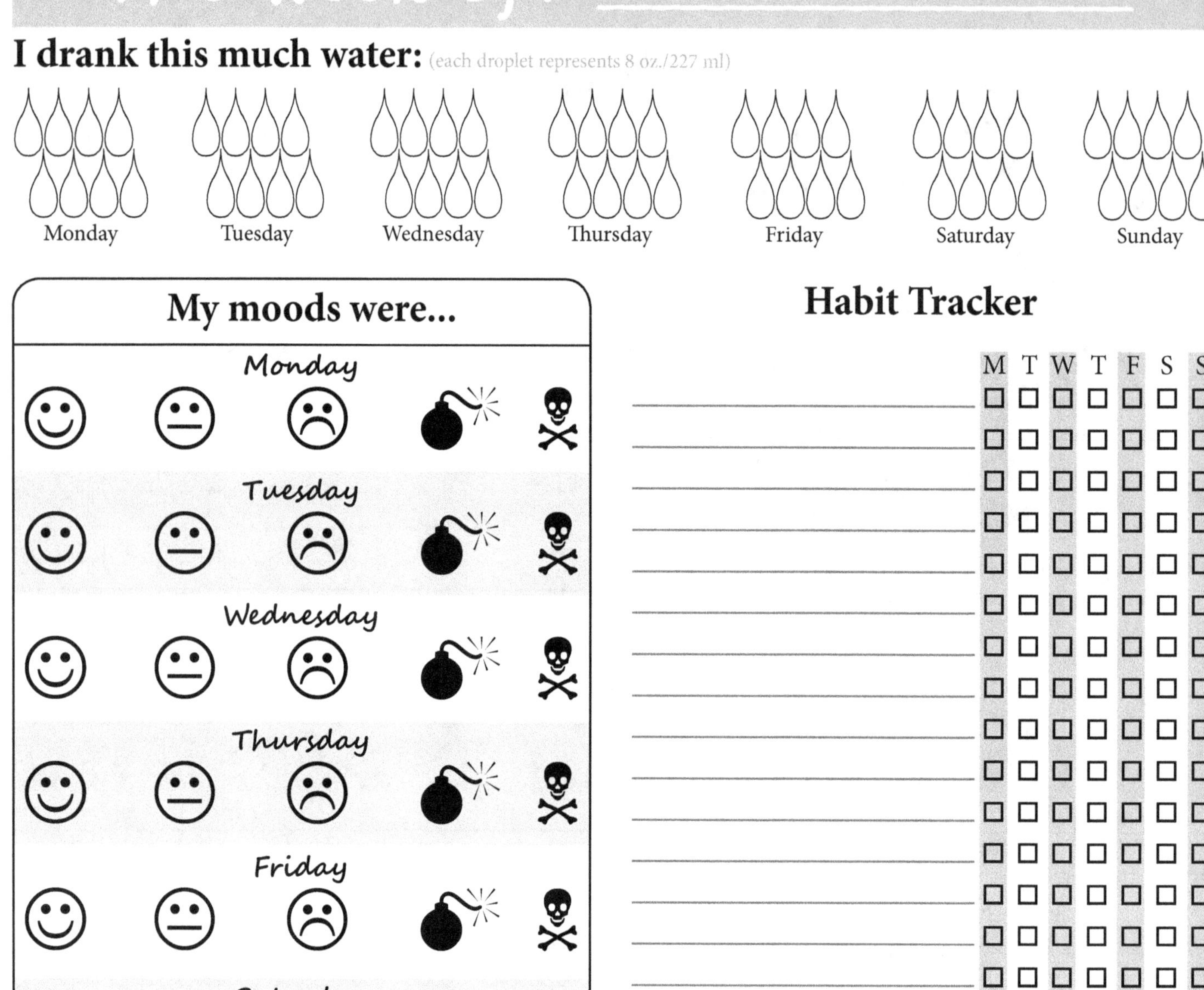

Monday

Tuesday

Wednesday

Thursday

Friday

Saturday

Sunday

Habit Tracker

M T W T F S S

Inspirations ❀ Affirmations ❀ Gratitudes

Sleep Tracker ✿ Week of _______

Hours Slept

M	T	W	T	F	S	S

12
11
10
9
8
7
6
5
4
3
2
1
0

Stuff I did before bed...

Energy Level

E — M — F
E — W — F
E — F — F
E — S — F
E — T — F
E — T — F
E — S — F

Dreams

M
T
W
T
F
S
S

Exercise Tracker

Type of Exercise	Amount	Notes	M	T	W	T	F	S	S
			☐	☐	☐	☐	☐	☐	☐
			☐	☐	☐	☐	☐	☐	☐
			☐	☐	☐	☐	☐	☐	☐
			☐	☐	☐	☐	☐	☐	☐
			☐	☐	☐	☐	☐	☐	☐
			☐	☐	☐	☐	☐	☐	☐
			☐	☐	☐	☐	☐	☐	☐
			☐	☐	☐	☐	☐	☐	☐
			☐	☐	☐	☐	☐	☐	☐
			☐	☐	☐	☐	☐	☐	☐

Food Tracker

Monday

Breakfast	
Lunch	
Dinner	
Snacks	

Tuesday

Breakfast	
Lunch	
Dinner	
Snacks	

Wednesday

Breakfast	
Lunch	
Dinner	
Snacks	

Thursday

Breakfast	
Lunch	
Dinner	
Snacks	

Friday

Breakfast	
Lunch	
Dinner	
Snacks	

Saturday

Breakfast	
Lunch	
Dinner	
Snacks	

Sunday

Breakfast	
Lunch	
Dinner	
Snacks	

Date: ________________________

Neck: ________________________

Chest: ________________________

Left Arm: ________________________

Right Arm: ________________________

Waist: ________________________

Hips: ________________________

Left Thigh: ________________________

Right Thigh: ________________________

Left Calf: ________________________

Right Calf: ________________________

Weight: ________________________

I drank this much water: (each droplet represents 8 oz./227 ml)

Monday Tuesday Wednesday Thursday Friday Saturday Sunday

My moods were...

Monday

Tuesday

Wednesday

Thursday

Friday

Saturday

Sunday

Habit Tracker

M T W T F S S

Inspirations ❀ *Affirmations* ❀ *Gratitudes*

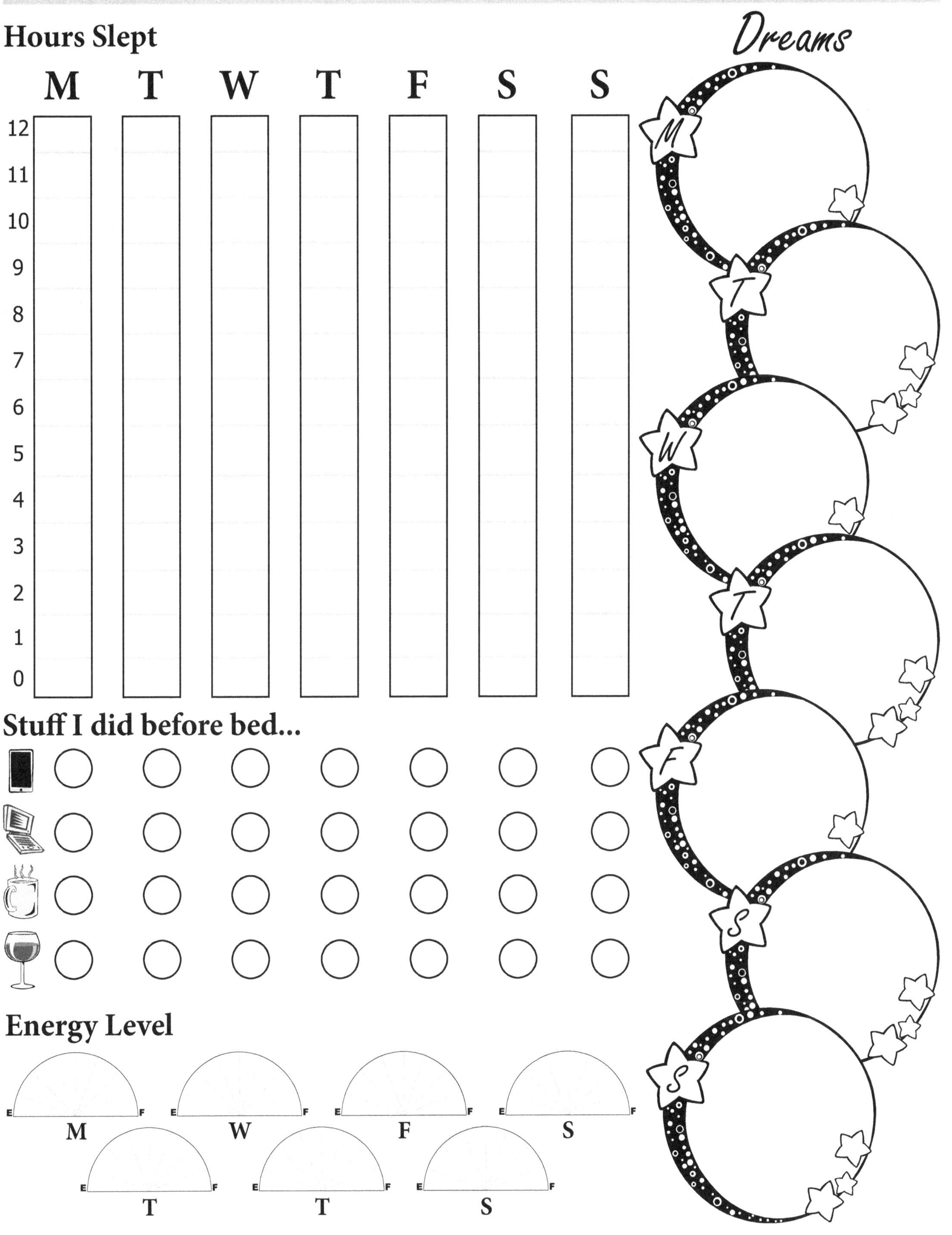

Sleep Tracker ❀ Week of ___________
Hours Slept
M T W T F S S
12
11
10
9
8
7
6
5
4
3
2
1
0
Dreams
M
T
W
T
F
S
S
Stuff I did before bed...
Energy Level
E F
M
E F
T
E F
W
E F
T
E F
F
E F
S
E F
S

Exercise Tracker

Type of Exercise	Amount	Notes	M	T	W	T	F	S	S
			☐	☐	☐	☐	☐	☐	☐
			☐	☐	☐	☐	☐	☐	☐
			☐	☐	☐	☐	☐	☐	☐
			☐	☐	☐	☐	☐	☐	☐
			☐	☐	☐	☐	☐	☐	☐
			☐	☐	☐	☐	☐	☐	☐
			☐	☐	☐	☐	☐	☐	☐
			☐	☐	☐	☐	☐	☐	☐
			☐	☐	☐	☐	☐	☐	☐
			☐	☐	☐	☐	☐	☐	☐

Food Tracker

Monday

Breakfast	
Lunch	
Dinner	
Snacks	

Tuesday

Breakfast	
Lunch	
Dinner	
Snacks	

Wednesday

Breakfast	
Lunch	
Dinner	
Snacks	

Thursday

Breakfast	
Lunch	
Dinner	
Snacks	

Friday

Breakfast	
Lunch	
Dinner	
Snacks	

Saturday

Breakfast	
Lunch	
Dinner	
Snacks	

Sunday

Breakfast	
Lunch	
Dinner	
Snacks	

Date: ___________________________

Neck: ___________________________

Chest: ___________________________

Left Arm: ___________________________

Right Arm: ___________________________

Waist: ___________________________

Hips: ___________________________

Left Thigh: ___________________________

Right Thigh: ___________________________

Left Calf: ___________________________

Right Calf: ___________________________

Weekly Weigh-In

Weight: ___________________________

I drank this much water: (each droplet represents 8 oz./227 ml)

Monday Tuesday Wednesday Thursday Friday Saturday Sunday

My moods were...

Monday

Tuesday

Wednesday

Thursday

Friday

Saturday

Sunday

Habit Tracker

M T W T F S S

Inspirations ❀ Affirmations ❀ Gratitudes

Sleep Tracker ❀ Week of _______________

Hours Slept

M	T	W	T	F	S	S

12
11
10
9
8
7
6
5
4
3
2
1
0

Dreams

M
T
W
T
F
S
S

Stuff I did before bed...

Energy Level

E — F M
E — F W
E — F F
E — F S
E — F T
E — F T
E — F S

Exercise Tracker

Type of Exercise	Amount	Notes	M	T	W	T	F	S	S
			☐	☐	☐	☐	☐	☐	☐
			☐	☐	☐	☐	☐	☐	☐
			☐	☐	☐	☐	☐	☐	☐
			☐	☐	☐	☐	☐	☐	☐
			☐	☐	☐	☐	☐	☐	☐
			☐	☐	☐	☐	☐	☐	☐
			☐	☐	☐	☐	☐	☐	☐
			☐	☐	☐	☐	☐	☐	☐
			☐	☐	☐	☐	☐	☐	☐
			☐	☐	☐	☐	☐	☐	☐

Food Tracker

Monday

Breakfast	
Lunch	
Dinner	
Snacks	

Tuesday

Breakfast	
Lunch	
Dinner	
Snacks	

Wednesday

Breakfast	
Lunch	
Dinner	
Snacks	

Thursday

Breakfast	
Lunch	
Dinner	
Snacks	

Friday

Breakfast	
Lunch	
Dinner	
Snacks	

Saturday

Breakfast	
Lunch	
Dinner	
Snacks	

Sunday

Breakfast	
Lunch	
Dinner	
Snacks	

Date: ___________________________________

Neck: ___________________________________

Chest: ___________________________________

Left Arm: ___________________________________

Right Arm: ___________________________________

Waist: ___________________________________

Hips: ___________________________________

Left Thigh: ___________________________________

Right Thigh: ___________________________________

Left Calf: ___________________________________

Right Calf: ___________________________________

Weekly Weigh-In

Weight: ___________________________________

I drank this much water: (each droplet represents 8 oz./227 ml)

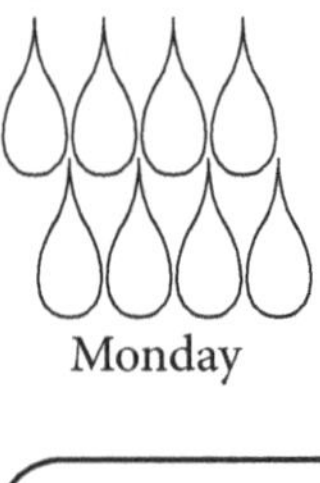  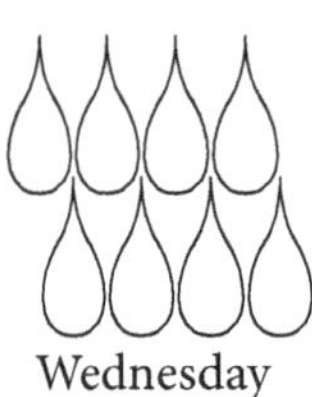 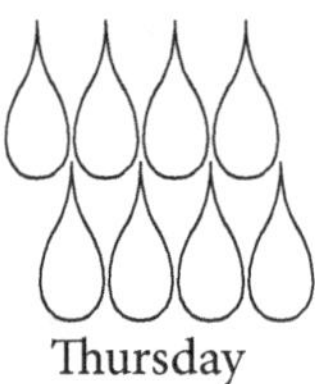   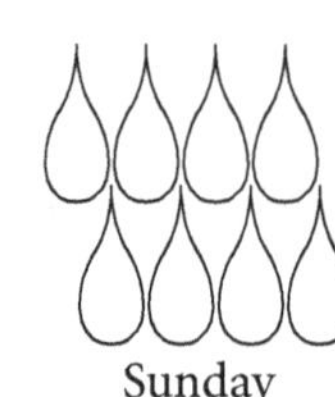

Monday	Tuesday	Wednesday	Thursday	Friday	Saturday	Sunday

My moods were...

Monday

Tuesday
 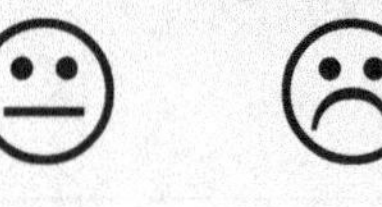  

Wednesday

Thursday

Friday

Saturday

Sunday

Habit Tracker

	M	T	W	T	F	S	S
____________	☐	☐	☐	☐	☐	☐	☐
____________	☐	☐	☐	☐	☐	☐	☐
____________	☐	☐	☐	☐	☐	☐	☐
____________	☐	☐	☐	☐	☐	☐	☐
____________	☐	☐	☐	☐	☐	☐	☐
____________	☐	☐	☐	☐	☐	☐	☐
____________	☐	☐	☐	☐	☐	☐	☐
____________	☐	☐	☐	☐	☐	☐	☐
____________	☐	☐	☐	☐	☐	☐	☐
____________	☐	☐	☐	☐	☐	☐	☐
____________	☐	☐	☐	☐	☐	☐	☐
____________	☐	☐	☐	☐	☐	☐	☐
____________	☐	☐	☐	☐	☐	☐	☐
____________	☐	☐	☐	☐	☐	☐	☐
____________	☐	☐	☐	☐	☐	☐	☐
____________	☐	☐	☐	☐	☐	☐	☐
____________	☐	☐	☐	☐	☐	☐	☐

Inspirations ❀ Affirmations ❀ Gratitudes

____

____

____

____

____

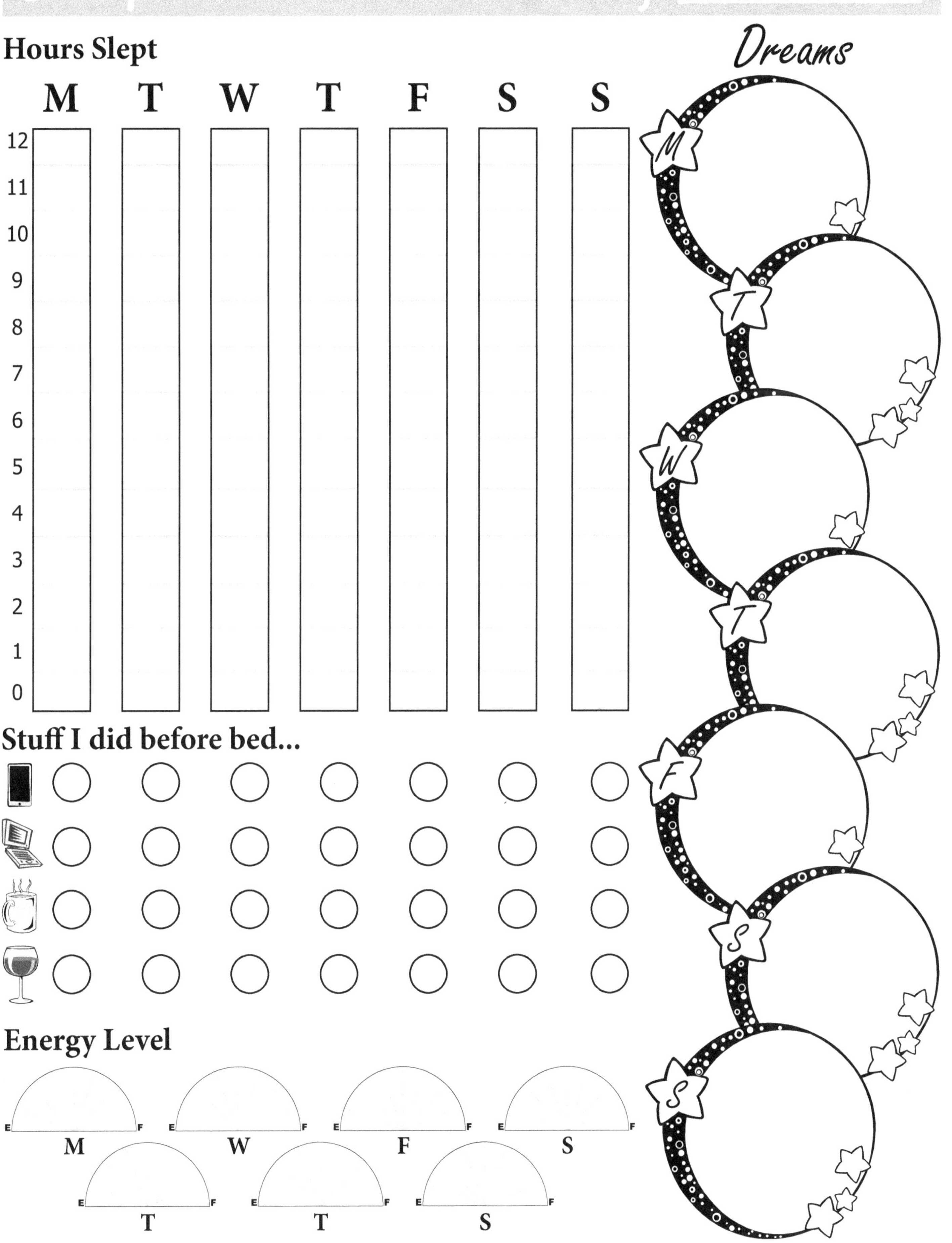

Sleep Tracker ❀ Week of ______

Hours Slept

Dreams

M T W T F S S

12
11
10
9
8
7
6
5
4
3
2
1
0

Stuff I did before bed...

Energy Level

E F
M
E F
T

E F
W
E F
T

E F
F
E F
S

E F
S

M
T
W
T
F
S
S

Exercise Tracker

Type of Exercise	Amount	Notes	M	T	W	T	F	S	S
			☐	☐	☐	☐	☐	☐	☐
			☐	☐	☐	☐	☐	☐	☐
			☐	☐	☐	☐	☐	☐	☐
			☐	☐	☐	☐	☐	☐	☐
			☐	☐	☐	☐	☐	☐	☐
			☐	☐	☐	☐	☐	☐	☐
			☐	☐	☐	☐	☐	☐	☐
			☐	☐	☐	☐	☐	☐	☐
			☐	☐	☐	☐	☐	☐	☐
			☐	☐	☐	☐	☐	☐	☐

Food Tracker

Monday

Breakfast	
Lunch	
Dinner	
Snacks	

Tuesday

Breakfast	
Lunch	
Dinner	
Snacks	

Wednesday

Breakfast	
Lunch	
Dinner	
Snacks	

Thursday

Breakfast	
Lunch	
Dinner	
Snacks	

Friday

Breakfast	
Lunch	
Dinner	
Snacks	

Saturday

Breakfast	
Lunch	
Dinner	
Snacks	

Sunday

Breakfast	
Lunch	
Dinner	
Snacks	

Date: _______________________

Neck: _______________________

Chest: _______________________

Left Arm: _______________________

Right Arm: _______________________

Waist: _______________________

Hips: _______________________

Left Thigh: _______________________

Right Thigh: _______________________

Left Calf: _______________________

Right Calf: _______________________

Weight: _______________________

I drank this much water: (each droplet represents 8 oz./227 ml)

| Monday | Tuesday | Wednesday | Thursday | Friday | Saturday | Sunday |

My moods were...

Monday

Tuesday

Wednesday

Thursday

Friday

Saturday

Sunday

Habit Tracker

M T W T F S S

Inspirations ❀ Affirmations ❀ Gratitudes

Sleep Tracker ✿ Week of _______

Hours Slept

M	T	W	T	F	S	S

12
11
10
9
8
7
6
5
4
3
2
1
0

Stuff I did before bed...

Energy Level

E — M — F
E — T — F
E — W — F
E — T — F
E — F — F
E — S — F
E — S — F

Dreams

M
T
W
T
F
S
S

Exercise Tracker

Type of Exercise	Amount	Notes	M	T	W	T	F	S	S
			☐	☐	☐	☐	☐	☐	☐
			☐	☐	☐	☐	☐	☐	☐
			☐	☐	☐	☐	☐	☐	☐
			☐	☐	☐	☐	☐	☐	☐
			☐	☐	☐	☐	☐	☐	☐
			☐	☐	☐	☐	☐	☐	☐
			☐	☐	☐	☐	☐	☐	☐
			☐	☐	☐	☐	☐	☐	☐
			☐	☐	☐	☐	☐	☐	☐
			☐	☐	☐	☐	☐	☐	☐

Food Tracker

Monday

Breakfast	
Lunch	
Dinner	
Snacks	

Tuesday

Breakfast	
Lunch	
Dinner	
Snacks	

Wednesday

Breakfast	
Lunch	
Dinner	
Snacks	

Thursday

Breakfast	
Lunch	
Dinner	
Snacks	

Friday

Breakfast	
Lunch	
Dinner	
Snacks	

Saturday

Breakfast	
Lunch	
Dinner	
Snacks	

Sunday

Breakfast	
Lunch	
Dinner	
Snacks	

Date: _______________________

Neck: _______________________

Chest: _______________________

Left Arm: _______________________

Right Arm: _______________________

Waist: _______________________

Hips: _______________________

Left Thigh: _______________________

Right Thigh: _______________________

Left Calf: _______________________

Right Calf: _______________________

Weekly Weigh-In

Weight: _______________________

I drank this much water: (each droplet represents 8 oz./227 ml)

Monday   Tuesday   Wednesday   Thursday   Friday   Saturday   Sunday

My moods were...

Monday

Tuesday

Wednesday

Thursday

Friday

Saturday

Sunday

Habit Tracker

M T W T F S S

Inspirations ❀ Affirmations ❀ Gratitudes

Sleep Tracker ❀ Week of _______

Hours Slept

M	T	W	T	F	S	S

12
11
10
9
8
7
6
5
4
3
2
1
0

Stuff I did before bed...

Energy Level

M   T   W   T   F   S   S

Dreams

M
T
W
T
F
S
S

Exercise Tracker

Type of Exercise	Amount	Notes	M	T	W	T	F	S	S
			☐	☐	☐	☐	☐	☐	☐
			☐	☐	☐	☐	☐	☐	☐
			☐	☐	☐	☐	☐	☐	☐
			☐	☐	☐	☐	☐	☐	☐
			☐	☐	☐	☐	☐	☐	☐
			☐	☐	☐	☐	☐	☐	☐
			☐	☐	☐	☐	☐	☐	☐
			☐	☐	☐	☐	☐	☐	☐
			☐	☐	☐	☐	☐	☐	☐
			☐	☐	☐	☐	☐	☐	☐

Food Tracker

Monday

Breakfast	
Lunch	
Dinner	
Snacks	

Tuesday

Breakfast	
Lunch	
Dinner	
Snacks	

Wednesday

Breakfast	
Lunch	
Dinner	
Snacks	

Thursday

Breakfast	
Lunch	
Dinner	
Snacks	

Friday

Breakfast	
Lunch	
Dinner	
Snacks	

Saturday

Breakfast	
Lunch	
Dinner	
Snacks	

Sunday

Breakfast	
Lunch	
Dinner	
Snacks	

Date: _______________________

Neck: _______________________

Chest: _______________________

Left Arm: _______________________

Right Arm: _______________________

Waist: _______________________

Hips: _______________________

Left Thigh: _______________________

Right Thigh: _______________________

Left Calf: _______________________

Right Calf: _______________________

Weekley Weigh-In

Weight: _______________________

I drank this much water: (each droplet represents 8 oz./227 ml)

Monday Tuesday Wednesday Thursday Friday Saturday Sunday

My moods were...

Monday

Tuesday

Wednesday

Thursday

Friday

Saturday

Sunday

Habit Tracker

M T W T F S S

Inspirations ❀ Affirmations ❀ Gratitudes

Sleep Tracker ❀ Week of ________

Dreams

Hours Slept

M	T	W	T	F	S	S

12
11
10
9
8
7
6
5
4
3
2
1
0

Stuff I did before bed...

Energy Level

M
T
W
T
F
S
S

E F

Exercise Tracker

Type of Exercise	Amount	Notes	M	T	W	T	F	S	S
			☐	☐	☐	☐	☐	☐	☐
			☐	☐	☐	☐	☐	☐	☐
			☐	☐	☐	☐	☐	☐	☐
			☐	☐	☐	☐	☐	☐	☐
			☐	☐	☐	☐	☐	☐	☐
			☐	☐	☐	☐	☐	☐	☐
			☐	☐	☐	☐	☐	☐	☐
			☐	☐	☐	☐	☐	☐	☐
			☐	☐	☐	☐	☐	☐	☐
			☐	☐	☐	☐	☐	☐	☐

Food Tracker

Monday

Breakfast	
Lunch	
Dinner	
Snacks	

Tuesday

Breakfast	
Lunch	
Dinner	
Snacks	

Wednesday

Breakfast	
Lunch	
Dinner	
Snacks	

Thursday

Breakfast	
Lunch	
Dinner	
Snacks	

Friday

Breakfast	
Lunch	
Dinner	
Snacks	

Saturday

Breakfast	
Lunch	
Dinner	
Snacks	

Sunday

Breakfast	
Lunch	
Dinner	
Snacks	

Date: ______________________________________

Neck: ______________________________________

Chest: ______________________________________

Left Arm: ______________________________________

Right Arm: ______________________________________

Waist: ______________________________________

Hips: ______________________________________

Left Thigh: ______________________________________

Right Thigh: ______________________________________

Left Calf: ______________________________________

Right Calf: ______________________________________

Weekly Weigh-In

Weight: ______________________________________

I drank this much water: (each droplet represents 8 oz./227 ml)

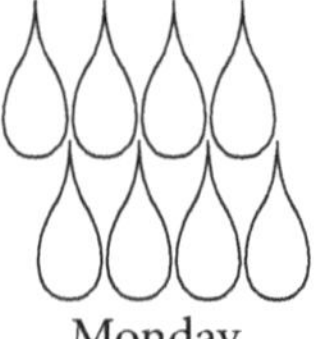

Monday

Tuesday

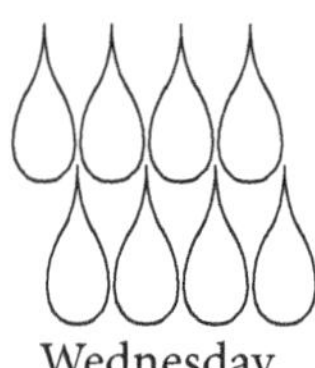

Wednesday

Thursday

Friday

Saturday

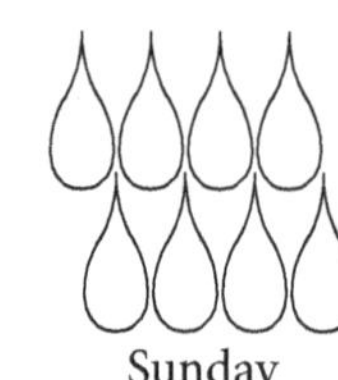

Sunday

My moods were...

Monday

Tuesday

Wednesday

Thursday

Friday

Saturday

Sunday

Habit Tracker

M T W T F S S

Inspirations ❀ Affirmations ❀ Gratitudes

Sleep Tracker ❀ Week of ________

Dreams

Hours Slept

M	T	W	T	F	S	S

12
11
10
9
8
7
6
5
4
3
2
1
0

Stuff I did before bed...

Energy Level

E — F M
E — F T
E — F W
E — F T
E — F F
E — F S
E — F S
E — F S

Exercise Tracker

Type of Exercise	Amount	Notes	M	T	W	T	F	S	S
			☐	☐	☐	☐	☐	☐	☐
			☐	☐	☐	☐	☐	☐	☐
			☐	☐	☐	☐	☐	☐	☐
			☐	☐	☐	☐	☐	☐	☐
			☐	☐	☐	☐	☐	☐	☐
			☐	☐	☐	☐	☐	☐	☐
			☐	☐	☐	☐	☐	☐	☐
			☐	☐	☐	☐	☐	☐	☐
			☐	☐	☐	☐	☐	☐	☐
			☐	☐	☐	☐	☐	☐	☐

Food Tracker

Monday

Breakfast	
Lunch	
Dinner	
Snacks	

Tuesday

Breakfast	
Lunch	
Dinner	
Snacks	

Wednesday

Breakfast	
Lunch	
Dinner	
Snacks	

Thursday

Breakfast	
Lunch	
Dinner	
Snacks	

Friday

Breakfast	
Lunch	
Dinner	
Snacks	

Saturday

Breakfast	
Lunch	
Dinner	
Snacks	

Sunday

Breakfast	
Lunch	
Dinner	
Snacks	

Date: _______________________

Neck: _______________________

Chest: _______________________

Left Arm: _______________________

Right Arm: _______________________

Waist: _______________________

Hips: _______________________

Left Thigh: _______________________

Right Thigh: _______________________

Left Calf: _______________________

Right Calf: _______________________

Weight: _______________________

I drank this much water: (each droplet represents 8 oz./227 ml)

Monday Tuesday Wednesday Thursday Friday Saturday Sunday

My moods were...

Monday

Tuesday

Wednesday

Thursday

Friday

Saturday

Sunday

Habit Tracker

M T W T F S S

Inspirations ❀ Affirmations ❀ Gratitudes

Sleep Tracker ❀ Week of _______

Hours Slept

	M	T	W	T	F	S	S
12							
11							
10							
9							
8							
7							
6							
5							
4							
3							
2							
1							
0							

Dreams

M
T
W
T
F
S
S

Stuff I did before bed...

Energy Level

M
T
W
T
F
S
S

The week of: _______________

Exercise Tracker

Type of Exercise	Amount	Notes	M	T	W	T	F	S	S
			☐	☐	☐	☐	☐	☐	☐
			☐	☐	☐	☐	☐	☐	☐
			☐	☐	☐	☐	☐	☐	☐
			☐	☐	☐	☐	☐	☐	☐
			☐	☐	☐	☐	☐	☐	☐
			☐	☐	☐	☐	☐	☐	☐
			☐	☐	☐	☐	☐	☐	☐
			☐	☐	☐	☐	☐	☐	☐
			☐	☐	☐	☐	☐	☐	☐
			☐	☐	☐	☐	☐	☐	☐

Food Tracker

Monday

Breakfast	
Lunch	
Dinner	
Snacks	

Tuesday

Breakfast	
Lunch	
Dinner	
Snacks	

Wednesday

Breakfast	
Lunch	
Dinner	
Snacks	

Thursday

Breakfast	
Lunch	
Dinner	
Snacks	

Friday

Breakfast	
Lunch	
Dinner	
Snacks	

Saturday

Breakfast	
Lunch	
Dinner	
Snacks	

Sunday

Breakfast	
Lunch	
Dinner	
Snacks	

Date: _______________________________

Neck: _______________________________

Chest: _______________________________

Left Arm: _______________________________

Right Arm: _______________________________

Waist: _______________________________

Hips: _______________________________

Left Thigh: _______________________________

Right Thigh: _______________________________

Left Calf: _______________________________

Right Calf: _______________________________

Weekly Weigh-In

Weight: _______________________________

I drank this much water: (each droplet represents 8 oz./227 ml)

Monday   Tuesday   Wednesday   Thursday   Friday   Saturday   Sunday

My moods were...

Monday

Tuesday

Wednesday

Thursday

Friday

Saturday

Sunday

Habit Tracker

M T W T F S S

Inspirations ✿ Affirmations ✿ Gratitudes

Sleep Tracker ❀ Week of ________

Hours Slept

| M | T | W | T | F | S | S |

12
11
10
9
8
7
6
5
4
3
2
1
0

Stuff I did before bed...

Energy Level

M T W T F S S

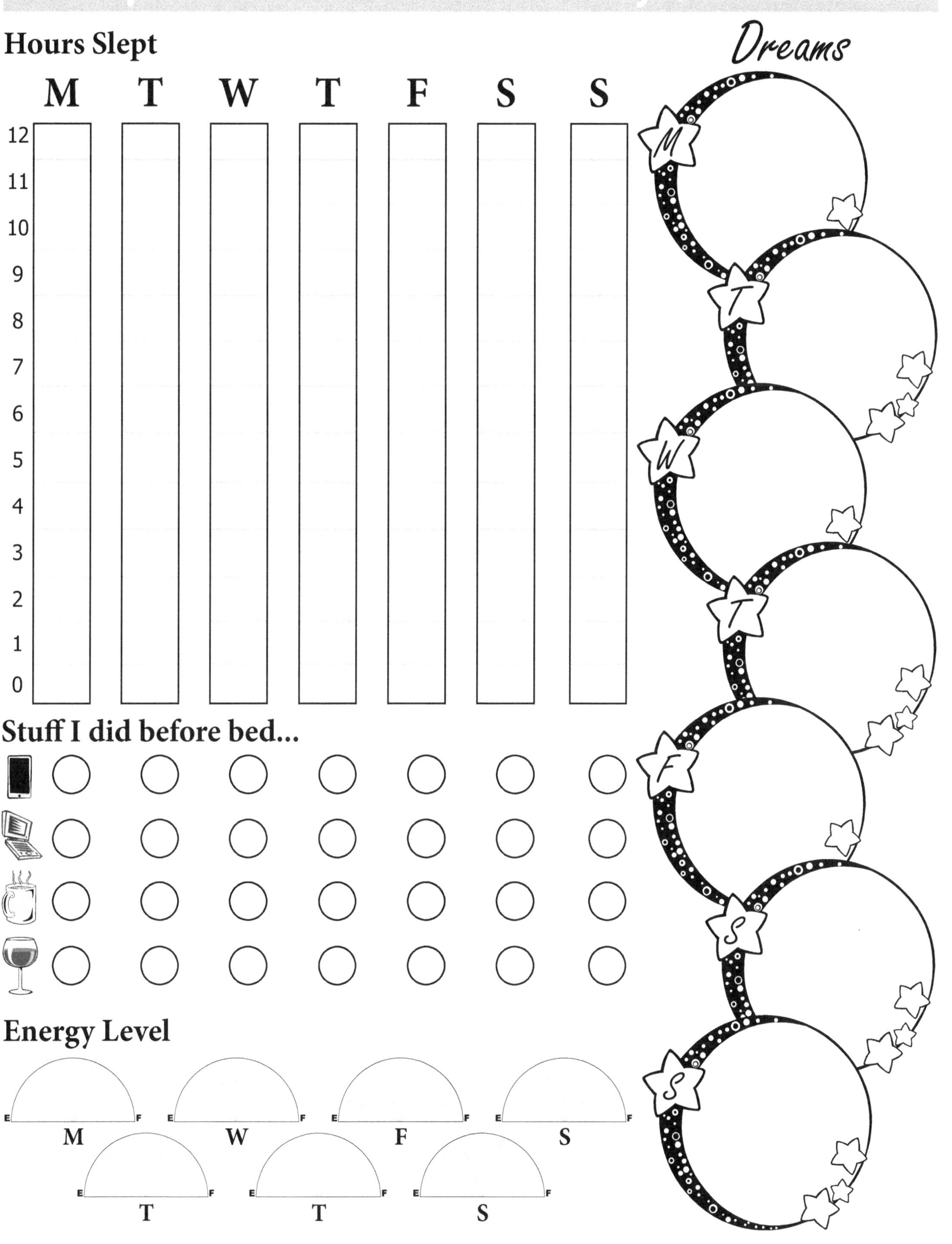

Exercise Tracker

Type of Exercise	Amount	Notes	M	T	W	T	F	S	S
			☐	☐	☐	☐	☐	☐	☐
			☐	☐	☐	☐	☐	☐	☐
			☐	☐	☐	☐	☐	☐	☐
			☐	☐	☐	☐	☐	☐	☐
			☐	☐	☐	☐	☐	☐	☐
			☐	☐	☐	☐	☐	☐	☐
			☐	☐	☐	☐	☐	☐	☐
			☐	☐	☐	☐	☐	☐	☐
			☐	☐	☐	☐	☐	☐	☐
			☐	☐	☐	☐	☐	☐	☐

Food Tracker

Monday

Breakfast	
Lunch	
Dinner	
Snacks	

Tuesday

Breakfast	
Lunch	
Dinner	
Snacks	

Wednesday

Breakfast	
Lunch	
Dinner	
Snacks	

Thursday

Breakfast	
Lunch	
Dinner	
Snacks	

Friday

Breakfast	
Lunch	
Dinner	
Snacks	

Saturday

Breakfast	
Lunch	
Dinner	
Snacks	

Sunday

Breakfast	
Lunch	
Dinner	
Snacks	

Date: _______________________________

Neck: _______________________________

Chest: _______________________________

Left Arm: _______________________________

Right Arm: _______________________________

Waist: _______________________________

Hips: _______________________________

Left Thigh: _______________________________

Right Thigh: _______________________________

Left Calf: _______________________________

Right Calf: _______________________________

Weight: _______________________________

I drank this much water: (each droplet represents 8 oz./227 ml)

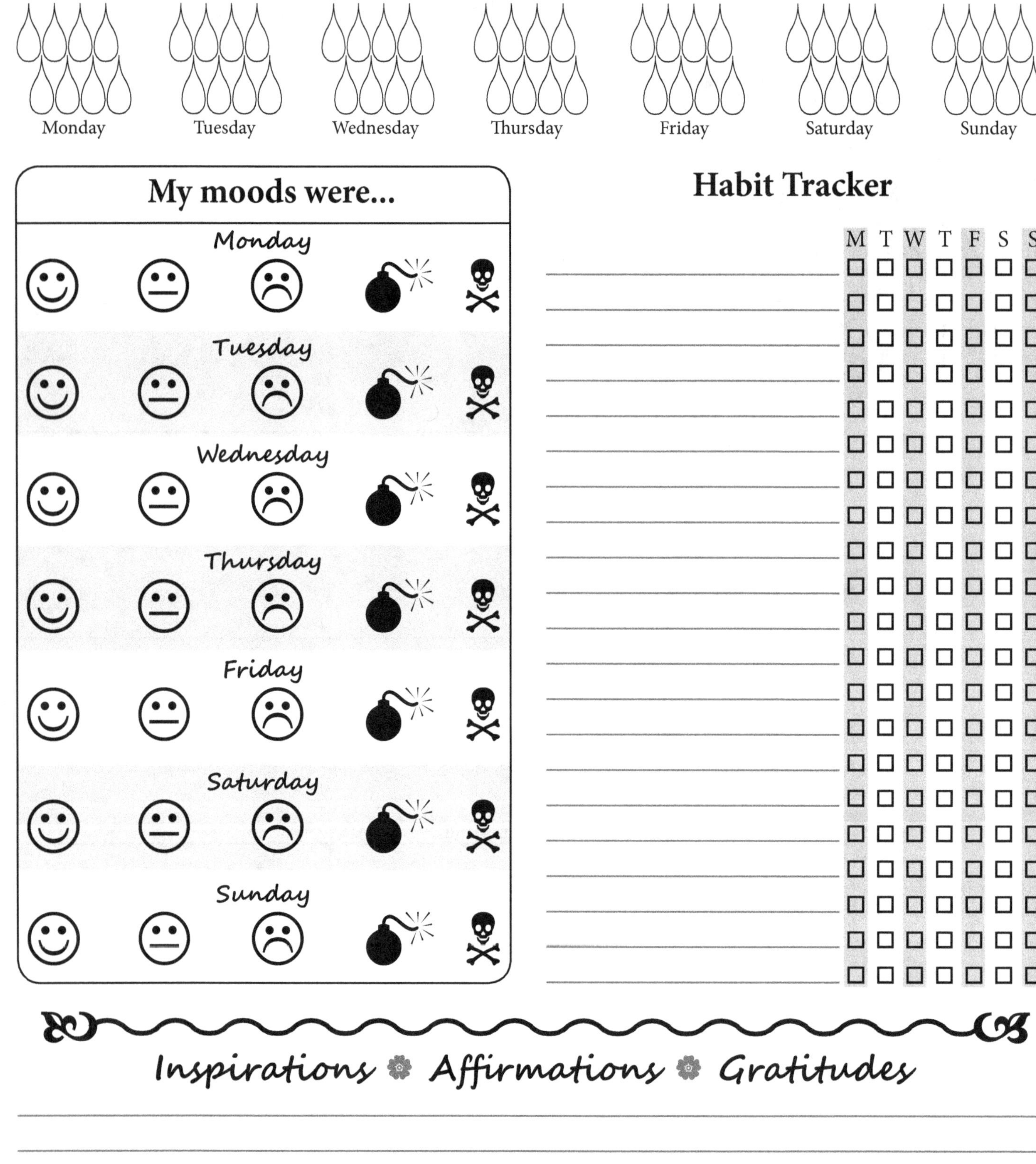

Monday   Tuesday   Wednesday   Thursday   Friday   Saturday   Sunday

My moods were...

Monday

Tuesday

Wednesday

Thursday

Friday

Saturday

Sunday

Habit Tracker

M T W T F S S

Inspirations ❀ Affirmations ❀ Gratitudes

Sleep Tracker ❀ Week of ___________

Hours Slept

M   T   W   T   F   S   S

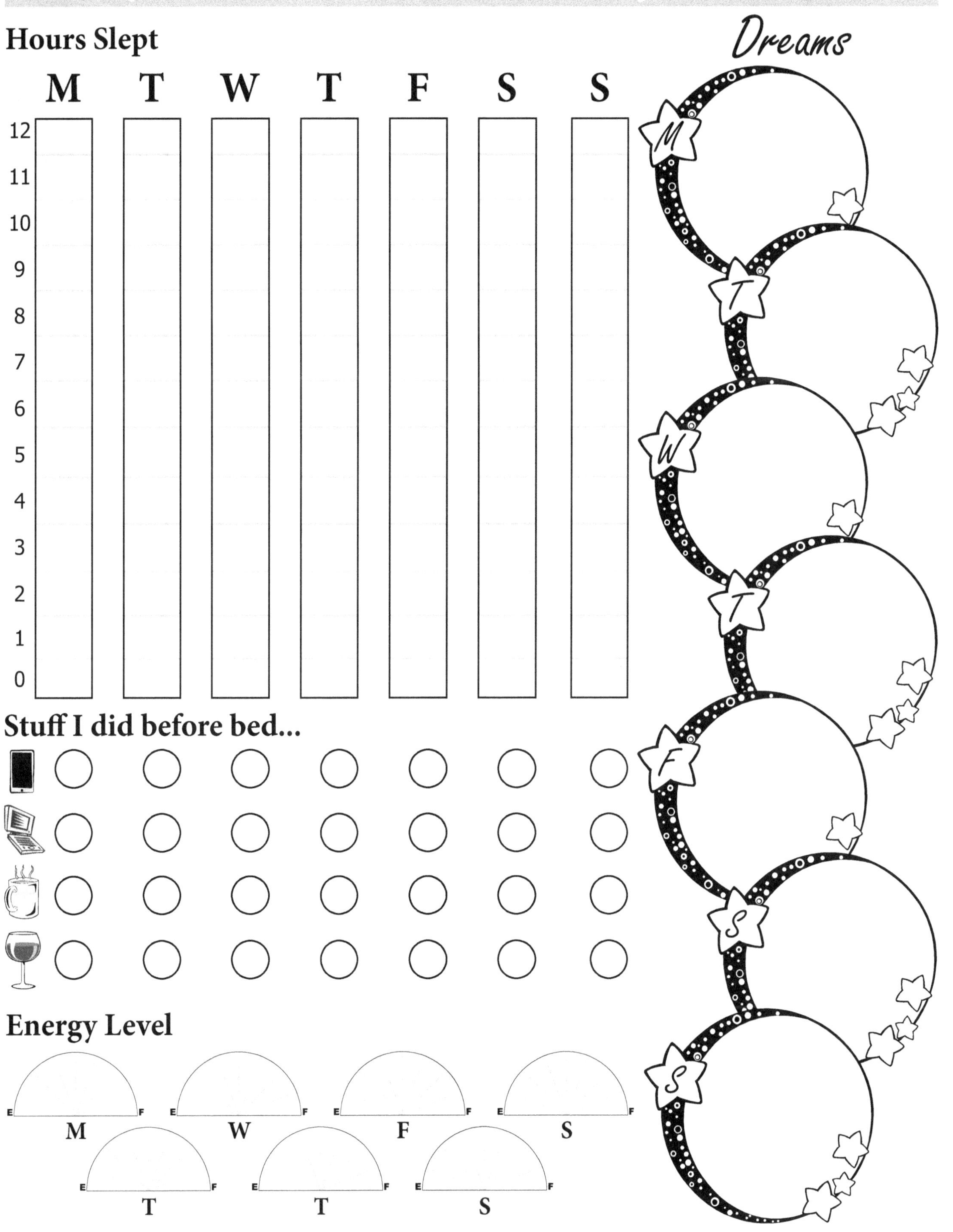

Dreams

Stuff I did before bed...

Energy Level

E — M — F

E — T — F

E — W — F

E — T — F

E — F — F

E — S — F

E — S — F

Exercise Tracker

Type of Exercise	Amount	Notes	M	T	W	T	F	S	S
			☐	☐	☐	☐	☐	☐	☐
			☐	☐	☐	☐	☐	☐	☐
			☐	☐	☐	☐	☐	☐	☐
			☐	☐	☐	☐	☐	☐	☐
			☐	☐	☐	☐	☐	☐	☐
			☐	☐	☐	☐	☐	☐	☐
			☐	☐	☐	☐	☐	☐	☐
			☐	☐	☐	☐	☐	☐	☐
			☐	☐	☐	☐	☐	☐	☐
			☐	☐	☐	☐	☐	☐	☐

Food Tracker

Monday

Breakfast	
Lunch	
Dinner	
Snacks	

Tuesday

Breakfast	
Lunch	
Dinner	
Snacks	

Wednesday

Breakfast	
Lunch	
Dinner	
Snacks	

Thursday

Breakfast	
Lunch	
Dinner	
Snacks	

Friday

Breakfast	
Lunch	
Dinner	
Snacks	

Saturday

Breakfast	
Lunch	
Dinner	
Snacks	

Sunday

Breakfast	
Lunch	
Dinner	
Snacks	

Date: _______________________________

Neck: _______________________________

Chest: _______________________________

Left Arm: _______________________________

Right Arm: _______________________________

Waist: _______________________________

Hips: _______________________________

Left Thigh: _______________________________

Right Thigh: _______________________________

Left Calf: _______________________________

Right Calf: _______________________________

Weight: _______________________________

I drank this much water: (each droplet represents 8 oz./227 ml)

Monday Tuesday Wednesday Thursday Friday Saturday Sunday

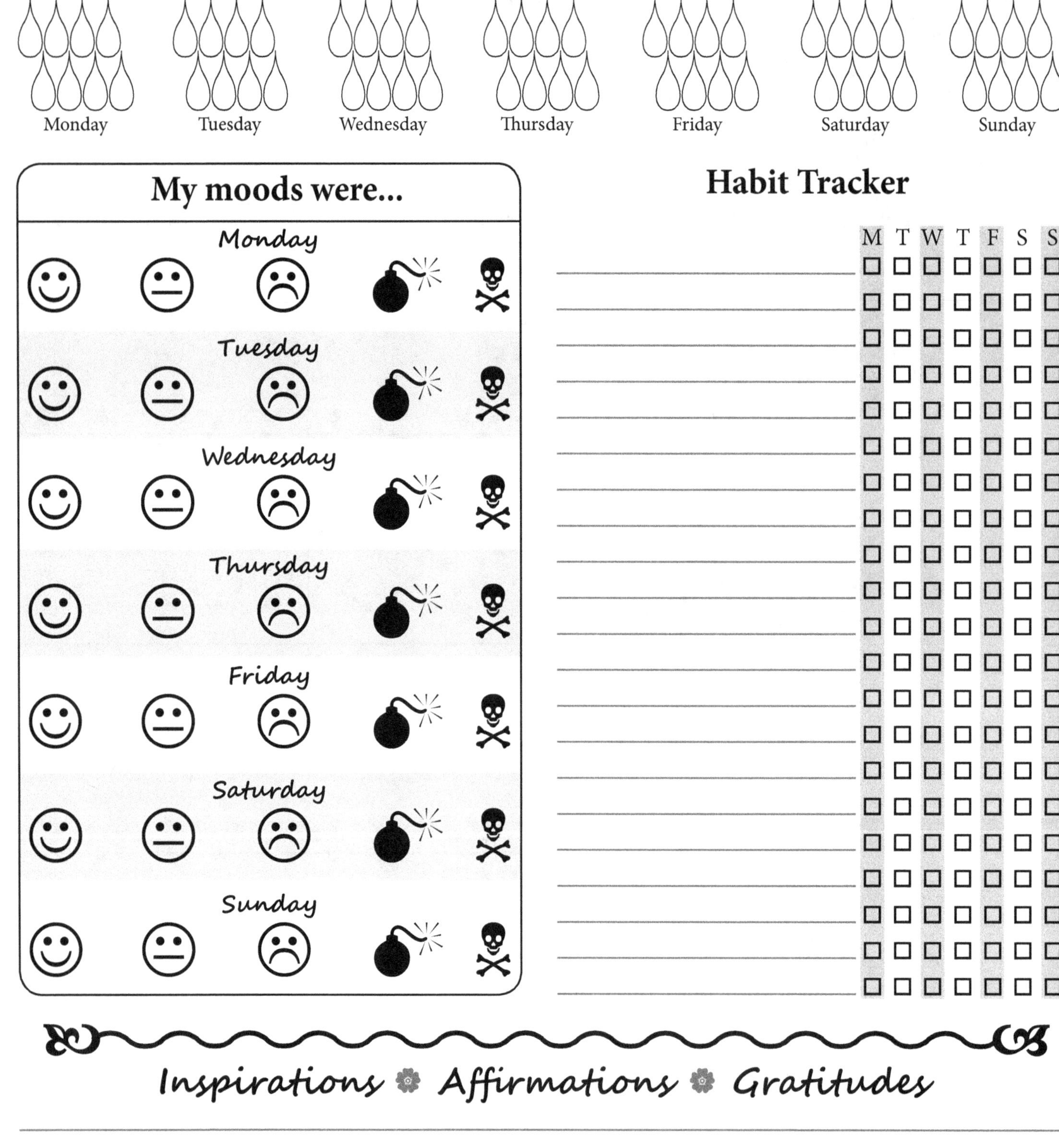

My moods were...

Monday

Tuesday

Wednesday

Thursday

Friday

Saturday

Sunday

Habit Tracker

M T W T F S S

Inspirations ❀ Affirmations ❀ Gratitudes

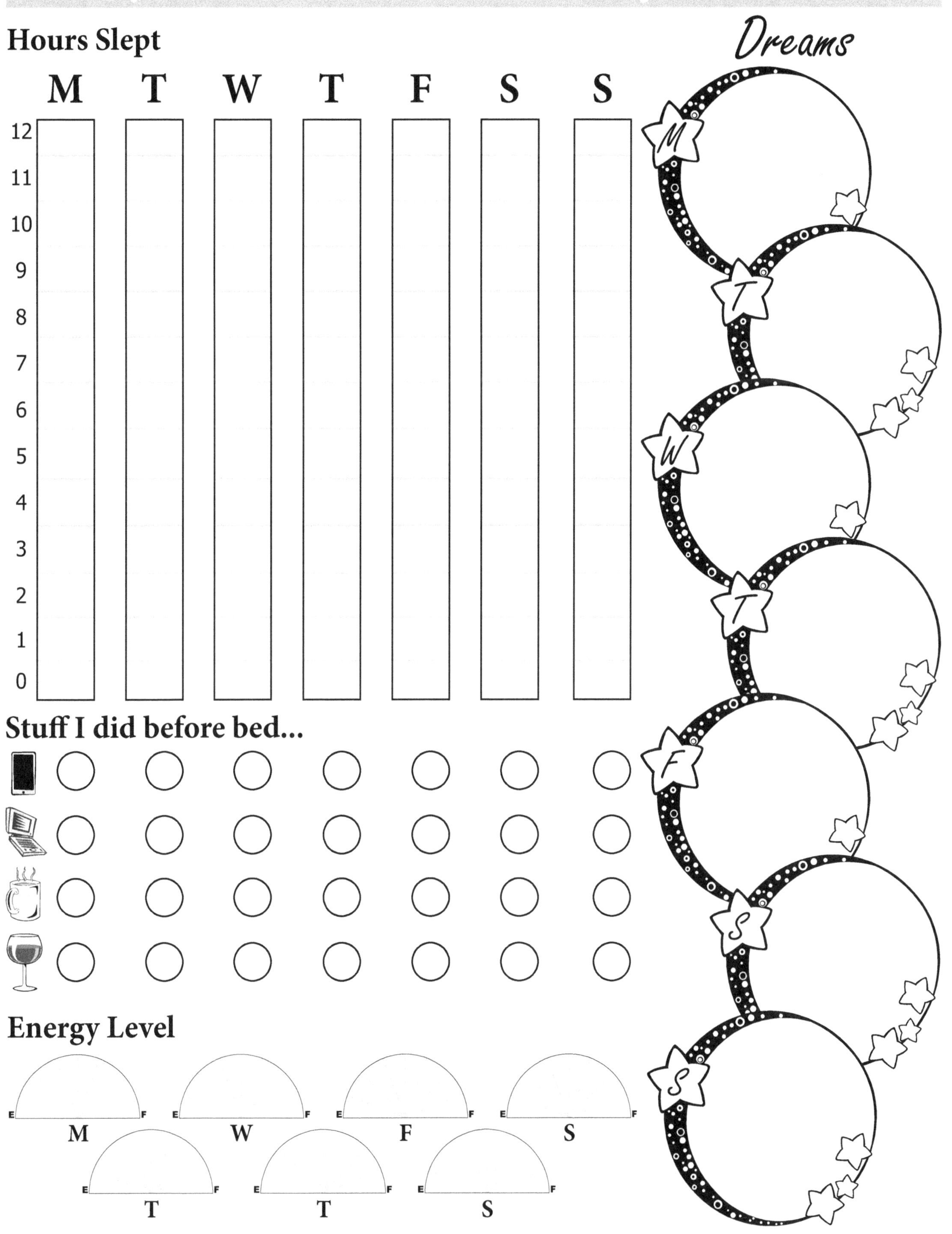

Sleep Tracker ❀ Week of __________
Hours Slept
M T W T F S S
Dreams
12
11
10
9
8
7
6
5
4
3
2
1
0
Stuff I did before bed...
Energy Level
E F E F E F E F
M W F S
E F E F E F
T T S
M
T
W
T
F
S
S

Exercise Tracker

Type of Exercise	Amount	Notes	M	T	W	T	F	S	S
			☐	☐	☐	☐	☐	☐	☐
			☐	☐	☐	☐	☐	☐	☐
			☐	☐	☐	☐	☐	☐	☐
			☐	☐	☐	☐	☐	☐	☐
			☐	☐	☐	☐	☐	☐	☐
			☐	☐	☐	☐	☐	☐	☐
			☐	☐	☐	☐	☐	☐	☐
			☐	☐	☐	☐	☐	☐	☐
			☐	☐	☐	☐	☐	☐	☐
			☐	☐	☐	☐	☐	☐	☐

Food Tracker

Monday

Breakfast	
Lunch	
Dinner	
Snacks	

Tuesday

Breakfast	
Lunch	
Dinner	
Snacks	

Wednesday

Breakfast	
Lunch	
Dinner	
Snacks	

Thursday

Breakfast	
Lunch	
Dinner	
Snacks	

Friday

Breakfast	
Lunch	
Dinner	
Snacks	

Saturday

Breakfast	
Lunch	
Dinner	
Snacks	

Sunday

Breakfast	
Lunch	
Dinner	
Snacks	

Date: ___________________________

Neck: ___________________________

Chest: ___________________________

Left Arm: ___________________________

Right Arm: ___________________________

Waist: ___________________________

Hips: ___________________________

Left Thigh: ___________________________

Right Thigh: ___________________________

Left Calf: ___________________________

Right Calf: ___________________________

Weekly Weigh-In

Weight: ___________________________

I drank this much water: (each droplet represents 8 oz./227 ml)

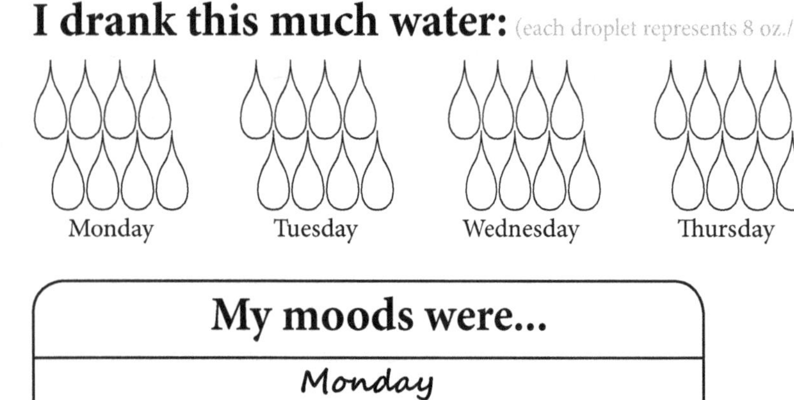

| Monday | Tuesday | Wednesday | Thursday | Friday | Saturday | Sunday |

My moods were...

Monday

Tuesday

Wednesday

Thursday

Friday

Saturday

Sunday

Habit Tracker

M T W T F S S

Inspirations ❀ Affirmations ❀ Gratitudes

____
____
____
____
____

Sleep Tracker ✿ Week of _______

Hours Slept

Dreams

| M | T | W | T | F | S | S |

12
11
10
9
8
7
6
5
4
3
2
1
0

Stuff I did before bed...

Energy Level

E — M — F
E — T — F
E — W — F
E — T — F
E — F — F
E — S — F
E — S — F

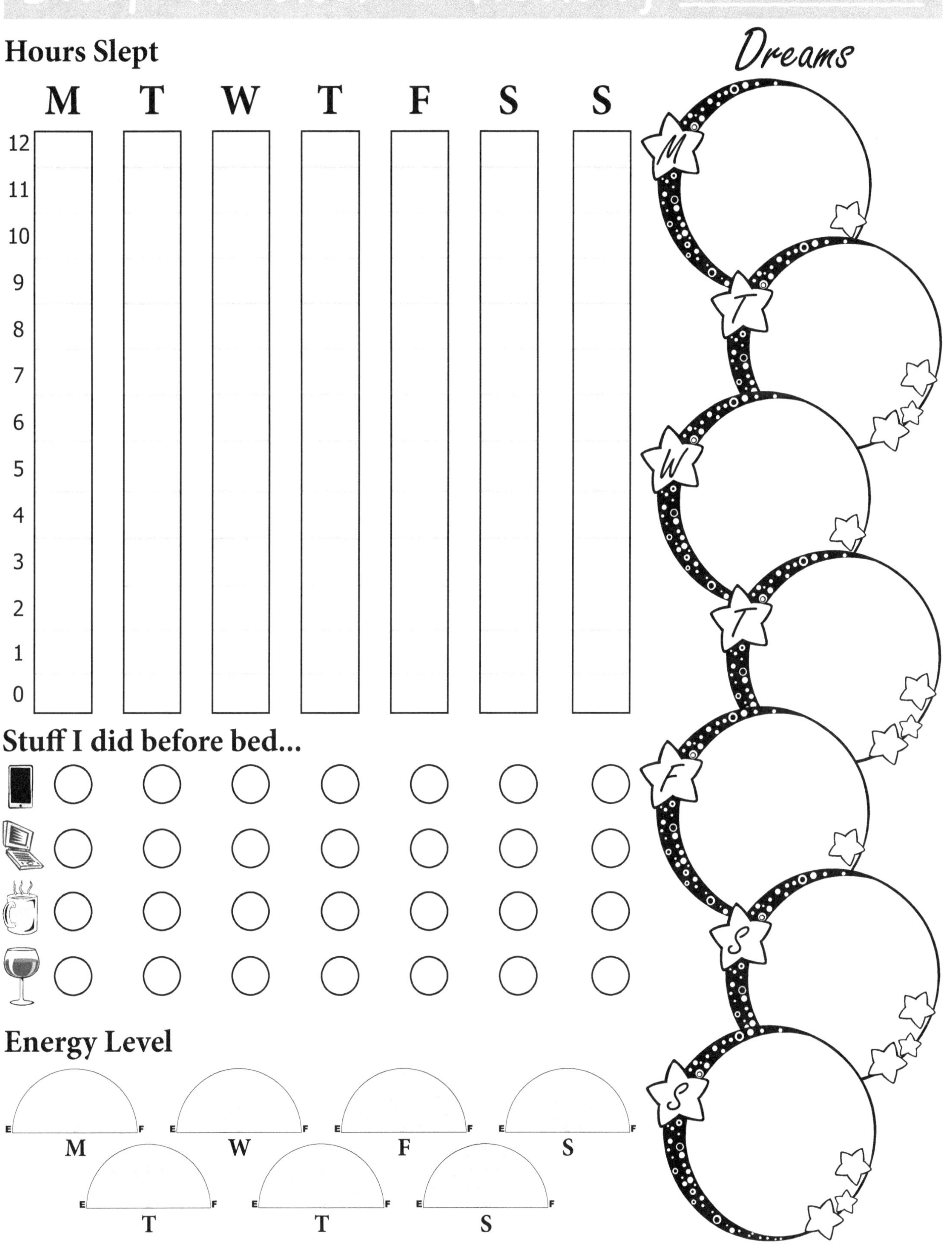

Exercise Tracker

Type of Exercise	Amount	Notes	M	T	W	T	F	S	S
			☐	☐	☐	☐	☐	☐	☐
			☐	☐	☐	☐	☐	☐	☐
			☐	☐	☐	☐	☐	☐	☐
			☐	☐	☐	☐	☐	☐	☐
			☐	☐	☐	☐	☐	☐	☐
			☐	☐	☐	☐	☐	☐	☐
			☐	☐	☐	☐	☐	☐	☐
			☐	☐	☐	☐	☐	☐	☐
			☐	☐	☐	☐	☐	☐	☐
			☐	☐	☐	☐	☐	☐	☐

Food Tracker

Monday

Breakfast	
Lunch	
Dinner	
Snacks	

Tuesday

Breakfast	
Lunch	
Dinner	
Snacks	

Wednesday

Breakfast	
Lunch	
Dinner	
Snacks	

Thursday

Breakfast	
Lunch	
Dinner	
Snacks	

Friday

Breakfast	
Lunch	
Dinner	
Snacks	

Saturday

Breakfast	
Lunch	
Dinner	
Snacks	

Sunday

Breakfast	
Lunch	
Dinner	
Snacks	

Date: ___________________________

Neck: ___________________________

Chest: ___________________________

Left Arm: ___________________________

Right Arm: ___________________________

Waist: ___________________________

Hips: ___________________________

Left Thigh: ___________________________

Right Thigh: ___________________________

Left Calf: ___________________________

Right Calf: ___________________________

Weight: ___________________________

I drank this much water: (each droplet represents 8 oz./227 ml)

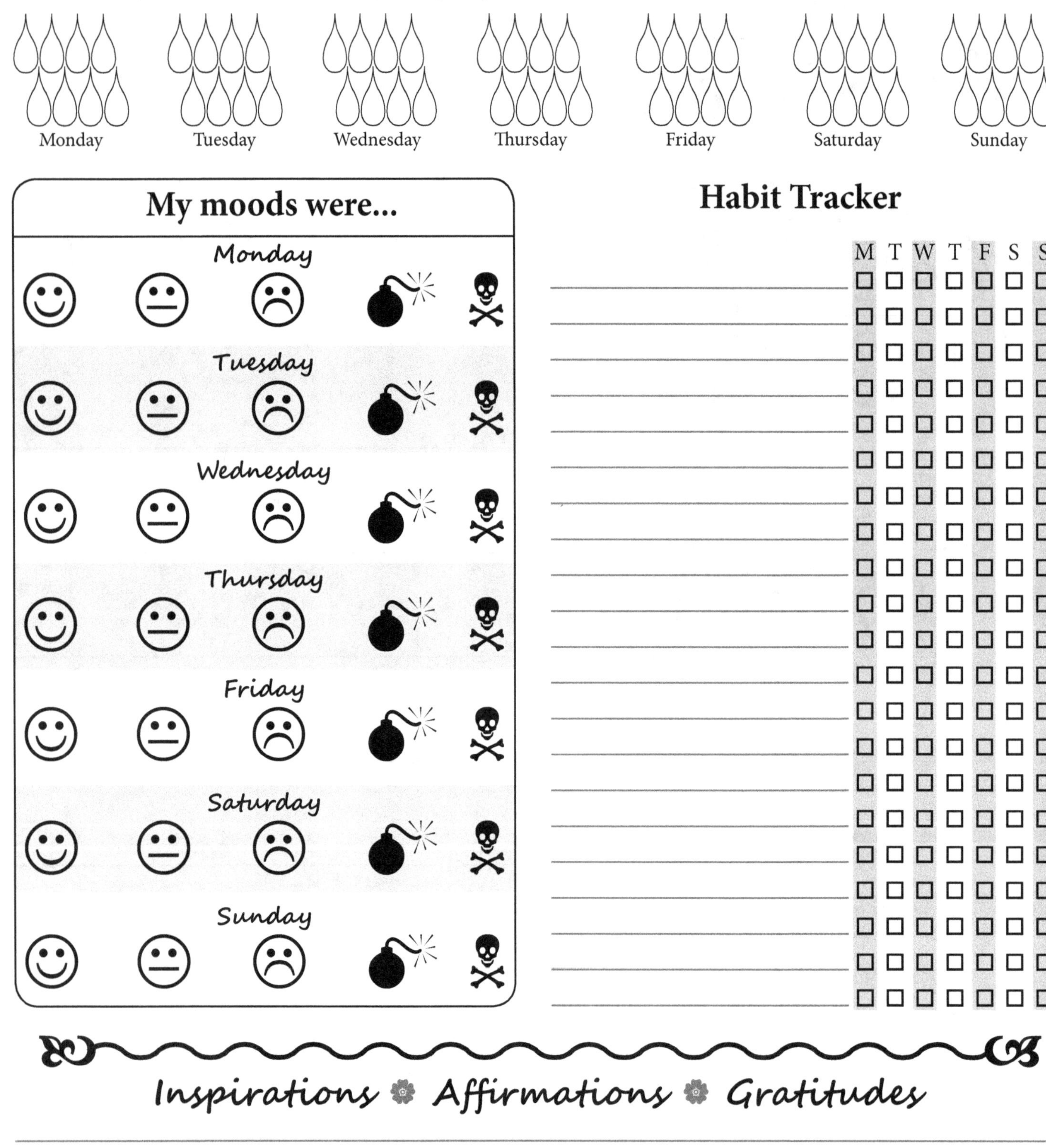

Inspirations ❀ Affirmations ❀ Gratitudes

Sleep Tracker ❀ Week of _______

Hours Slept

	M	T	W	T	F	S	S

12
11
10
9
8
7
6
5
4
3
2
1
0

Stuff I did before bed...

Energy Level

M T W T F S S

Dreams

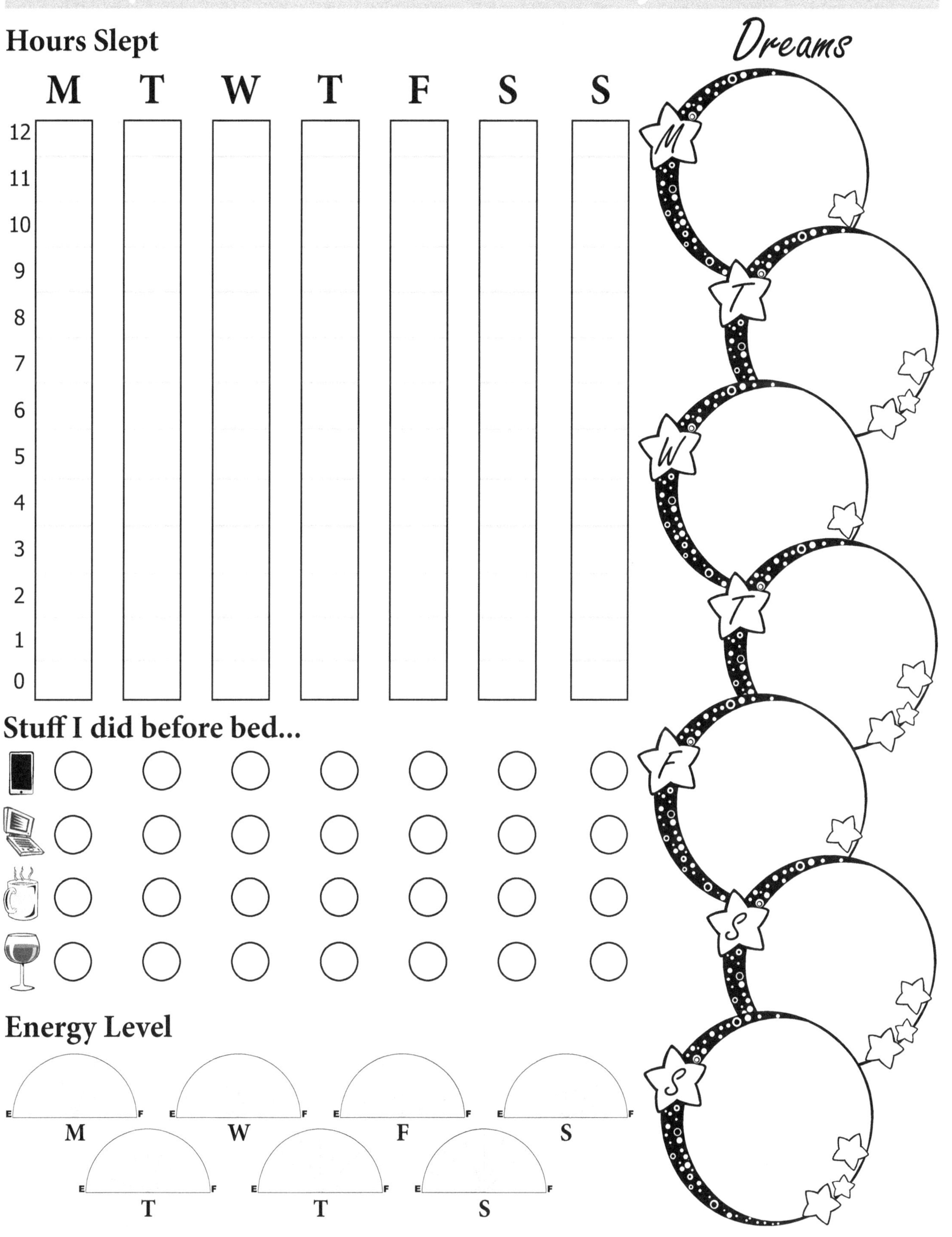

Exercise Tracker

Type of Exercise	Amount	Notes	M	T	W	T	F	S	S
			☐	☐	☐	☐	☐	☐	☐
			☐	☐	☐	☐	☐	☐	☐
			☐	☐	☐	☐	☐	☐	☐
			☐	☐	☐	☐	☐	☐	☐
			☐	☐	☐	☐	☐	☐	☐
			☐	☐	☐	☐	☐	☐	☐
			☐	☐	☐	☐	☐	☐	☐
			☐	☐	☐	☐	☐	☐	☐
			☐	☐	☐	☐	☐	☐	☐
			☐	☐	☐	☐	☐	☐	☐

Food Tracker

Monday

Breakfast	
Lunch	
Dinner	
Snacks	

Tuesday

Breakfast	
Lunch	
Dinner	
Snacks	

Wednesday

Breakfast	
Lunch	
Dinner	
Snacks	

Thursday

Breakfast	
Lunch	
Dinner	
Snacks	

Friday

Breakfast	
Lunch	
Dinner	
Snacks	

Saturday

Breakfast	
Lunch	
Dinner	
Snacks	

Sunday

Breakfast	
Lunch	
Dinner	
Snacks	

Date: _______________________

Neck: _______________________

Chest: _______________________

Left Arm: _______________________

Right Arm: _______________________

Waist: _______________________

Hips: _______________________

Left Thigh: _______________________

Right Thigh: _______________________

Left Calf: _______________________

Right Calf: _______________________

Weekly Weigh-In

Weight: _______________________

I drank this much water: (each droplet represents 8 oz./227 ml)

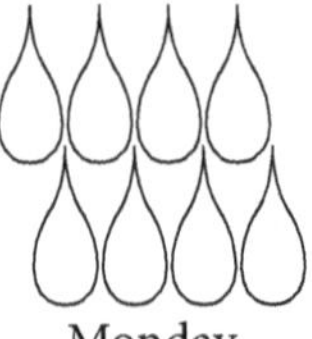 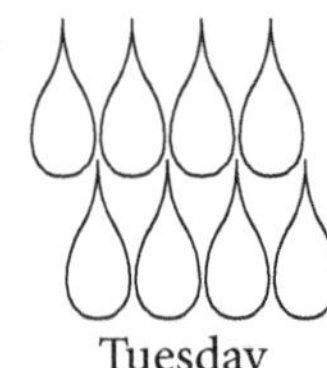 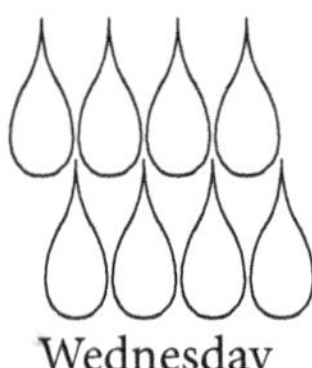 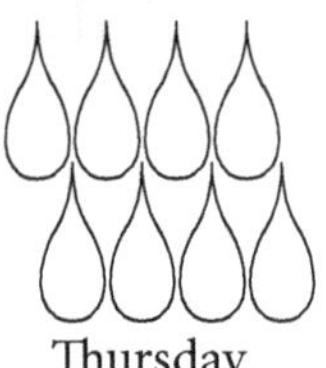  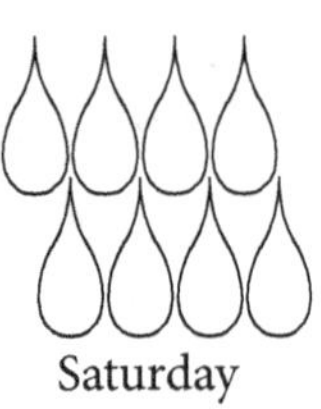 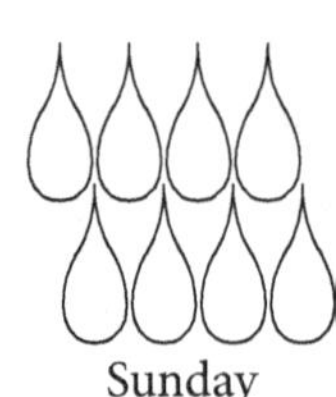

| Monday | Tuesday | Wednesday | Thursday | Friday | Saturday | Sunday |

My moods were...

Monday

Tuesday

Wednesday

Thursday

Friday
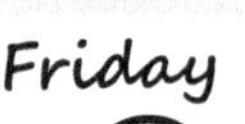    

Saturday

Sunday

Habit Tracker

	M	T	W	T	F	S	S
________	☐	☐	☐	☐	☐	☐	☐
________	☐	☐	☐	☐	☐	☐	☐
________	☐	☐	☐	☐	☐	☐	☐
________	☐	☐	☐	☐	☐	☐	☐
________	☐	☐	☐	☐	☐	☐	☐
________	☐	☐	☐	☐	☐	☐	☐
________	☐	☐	☐	☐	☐	☐	☐
________	☐	☐	☐	☐	☐	☐	☐
________	☐	☐	☐	☐	☐	☐	☐
________	☐	☐	☐	☐	☐	☐	☐
________	☐	☐	☐	☐	☐	☐	☐
________	☐	☐	☐	☐	☐	☐	☐
________	☐	☐	☐	☐	☐	☐	☐
________	☐	☐	☐	☐	☐	☐	☐
________	☐	☐	☐	☐	☐	☐	☐
________	☐	☐	☐	☐	☐	☐	☐

Inspirations ❀ Affirmations ❀ Gratitudes

____

____

____

____

____

Sleep Tracker ✿ Week of ________

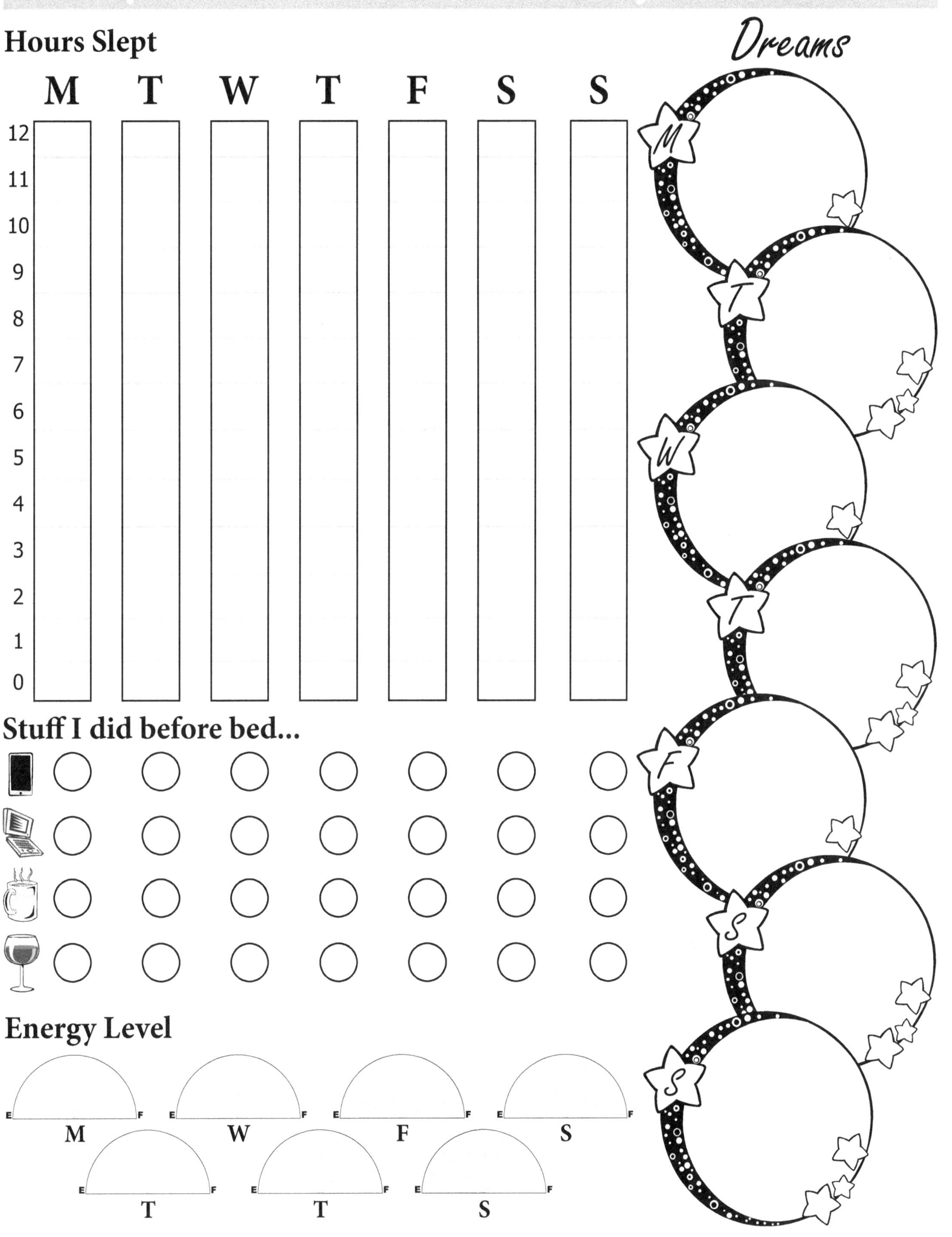

Exercise Tracker

Type of Exercise	Amount	Notes	M	T	W	T	F	S	S
			☐	☐	☐	☐	☐	☐	☐
			☐	☐	☐	☐	☐	☐	☐
			☐	☐	☐	☐	☐	☐	☐
			☐	☐	☐	☐	☐	☐	☐
			☐	☐	☐	☐	☐	☐	☐
			☐	☐	☐	☐	☐	☐	☐
			☐	☐	☐	☐	☐	☐	☐
			☐	☐	☐	☐	☐	☐	☐
			☐	☐	☐	☐	☐	☐	☐
			☐	☐	☐	☐	☐	☐	☐

Food Tracker

Monday

Breakfast	
Lunch	
Dinner	
Snacks	

Tuesday

Breakfast	
Lunch	
Dinner	
Snacks	

Wednesday

Breakfast	
Lunch	
Dinner	
Snacks	

Thursday

Breakfast	
Lunch	
Dinner	
Snacks	

Friday

Breakfast	
Lunch	
Dinner	
Snacks	

Saturday

Breakfast	
Lunch	
Dinner	
Snacks	

Sunday

Breakfast	
Lunch	
Dinner	
Snacks	

Date: ___________________________

Neck: ___________________________

Chest: ___________________________

Left Arm: ___________________________

Right Arm: ___________________________

Waist: ___________________________

Hips: ___________________________

Left Thigh: ___________________________

Right Thigh: ___________________________

Left Calf: ___________________________

Right Calf: ___________________________

Weekly Weigh-In

Weight: ___________________________

I drank this much water: (each droplet represents 8 oz./227 ml)

Monday Tuesday Wednesday Thursday Friday Saturday Sunday

My moods were...

Monday

Tuesday

Wednesday

Thursday

Friday

Saturday

Sunday

Habit Tracker

M T W T F S S

Inspirations ❀ Affirmations ❀ Gratitudes

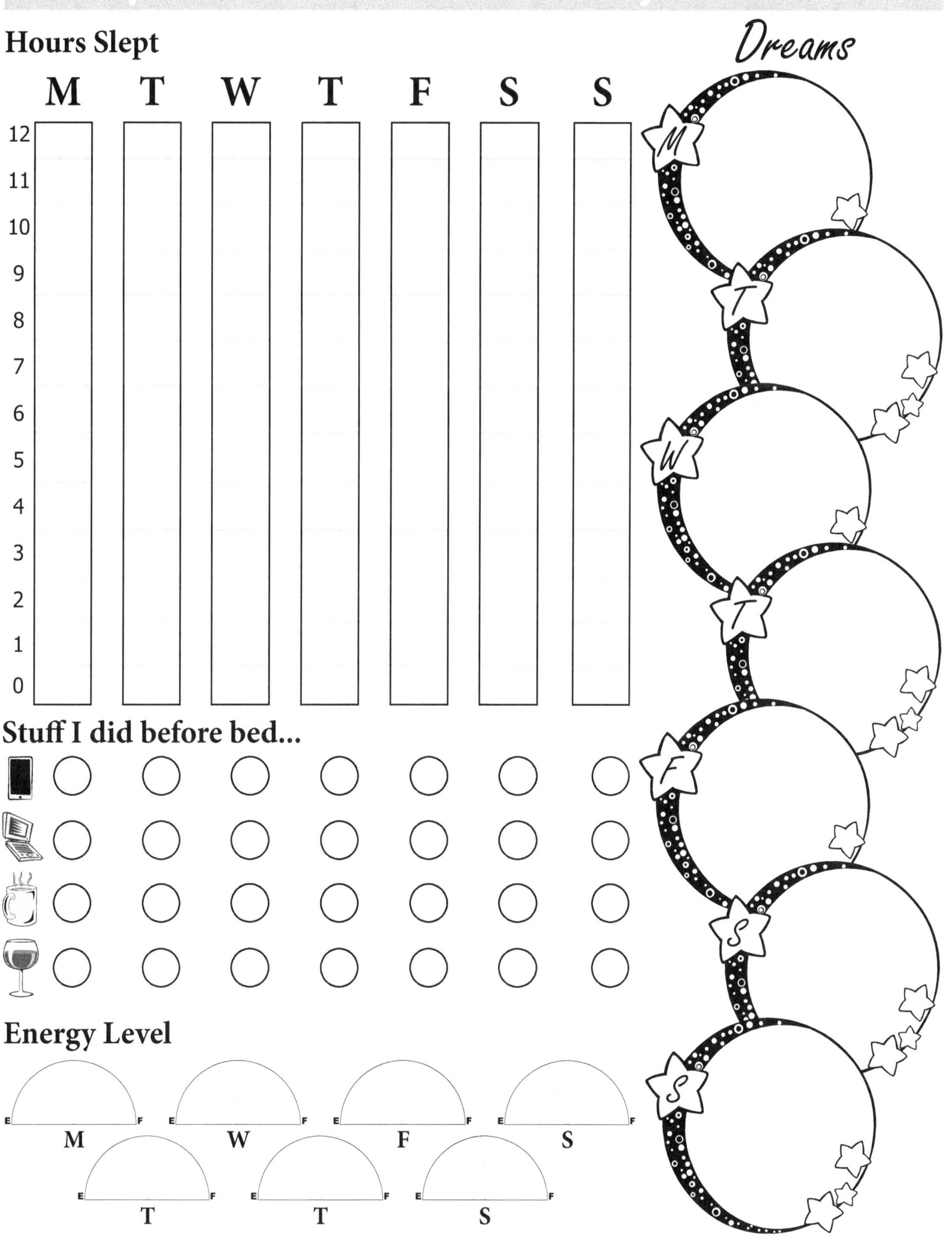

Sleep Tracker ❀ Week of ______
Hours Slept
Dreams
M T W T F S S
12
11
10
9
8
7
6
5
4
3
2
1
0
Stuff I did before bed...
Energy Level
E F
M
E F
T
E F
W
E F
T
E F
F
E F
S
E F
S
M
T
W
T
F
S
S

Exercise Tracker

Type of Exercise	Amount	Notes	M	T	W	T	F	S	S
			☐	☐	☐	☐	☐	☐	☐
			☐	☐	☐	☐	☐	☐	☐
			☐	☐	☐	☐	☐	☐	☐
			☐	☐	☐	☐	☐	☐	☐
			☐	☐	☐	☐	☐	☐	☐
			☐	☐	☐	☐	☐	☐	☐
			☐	☐	☐	☐	☐	☐	☐
			☐	☐	☐	☐	☐	☐	☐
			☐	☐	☐	☐	☐	☐	☐
			☐	☐	☐	☐	☐	☐	☐

Food Tracker

Monday

Breakfast	
Lunch	
Dinner	
Snacks	

Tuesday

Breakfast	
Lunch	
Dinner	
Snacks	

Wednesday

Breakfast	
Lunch	
Dinner	
Snacks	

Thursday

Breakfast	
Lunch	
Dinner	
Snacks	

Friday

Breakfast	
Lunch	
Dinner	
Snacks	

Saturday

Breakfast	
Lunch	
Dinner	
Snacks	

Sunday

Breakfast	
Lunch	
Dinner	
Snacks	

Date: _______________________

Neck: _______________________

Chest: _______________________

Left Arm: _______________________

Right Arm: _______________________

Waist: _______________________

Hips: _______________________

Left Thigh: _______________________

Right Thigh: _______________________

Left Calf: _______________________

Right Calf: _______________________

Weight: _______________________

I drank this much water: (each droplet represents 8 oz./227 ml)

Monday   Tuesday   Wednesday   Thursday   Friday   Saturday   Sunday

My moods were...

Monday

Tuesday

Wednesday

Thursday

Friday

Saturday

Sunday

Habit Tracker

M T W T F S S

Inspirations ❀ Affirmations ❀ Gratitudes

Sleep Tracker ❀ Week of __________

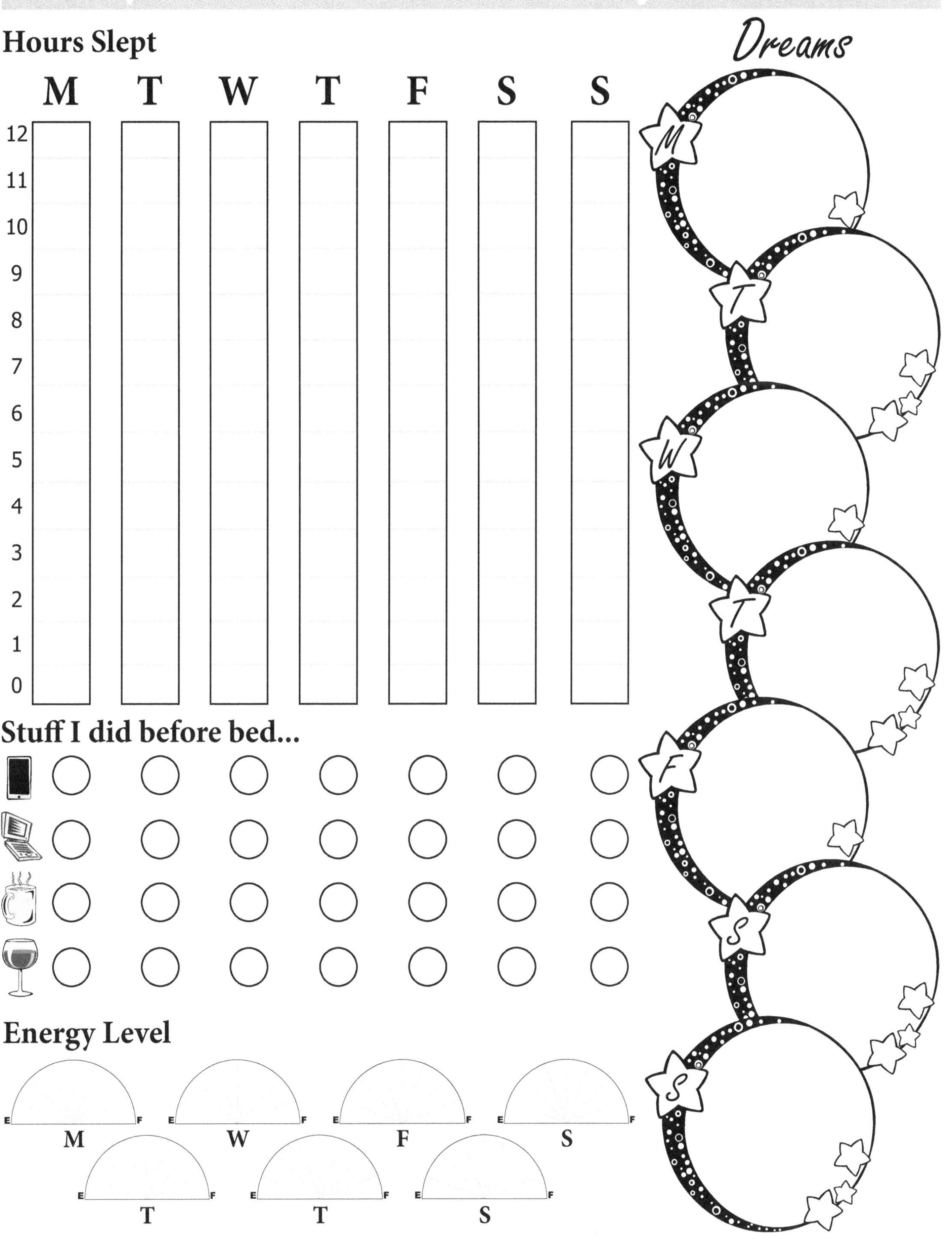

Hours Slept

| M | T | W | T | F | S | S |

12
11
10
9
8
7
6
5
4
3
2
1
0

Dreams

Stuff I did before bed...

Energy Level

E F M
E F T
E F W
E F T
E F F
E F S
E F S
E F S

The week of: _______________

Exercise Tracker

Type of Exercise	Amount	Notes	M	T	W	T	F	S	S
			☐	☐	☐	☐	☐	☐	☐
			☐	☐	☐	☐	☐	☐	☐
			☐	☐	☐	☐	☐	☐	☐
			☐	☐	☐	☐	☐	☐	☐
			☐	☐	☐	☐	☐	☐	☐
			☐	☐	☐	☐	☐	☐	☐
			☐	☐	☐	☐	☐	☐	☐
			☐	☐	☐	☐	☐	☐	☐
			☐	☐	☐	☐	☐	☐	☐
			☐	☐	☐	☐	☐	☐	☐

Food Tracker

Monday

Breakfast	
Lunch	
Dinner	
Snacks	

Tuesday

Breakfast	
Lunch	
Dinner	
Snacks	

Wednesday

Breakfast	
Lunch	
Dinner	
Snacks	

Thursday

Breakfast	
Lunch	
Dinner	
Snacks	

Friday

Breakfast	
Lunch	
Dinner	
Snacks	

Saturday

Breakfast	
Lunch	
Dinner	
Snacks	

Sunday

Breakfast	
Lunch	
Dinner	
Snacks	

Date: ___________________________________

Neck: _____________________________________

Chest: ____________________________________

Left Arm: __________________________________

Right Arm: _________________________________

Waist: ____________________________________

Hips: _____________________________________

Left Thigh: ________________________________

Right Thigh: _______________________________

Left Calf: _________________________________

Right Calf: ________________________________

Weekly Weigh-In

Weight: ___________________________________

I drank this much water: (each droplet represents 8 oz./227 ml)

Monday Tuesday Wednesday Thursday Friday Saturday Sunday

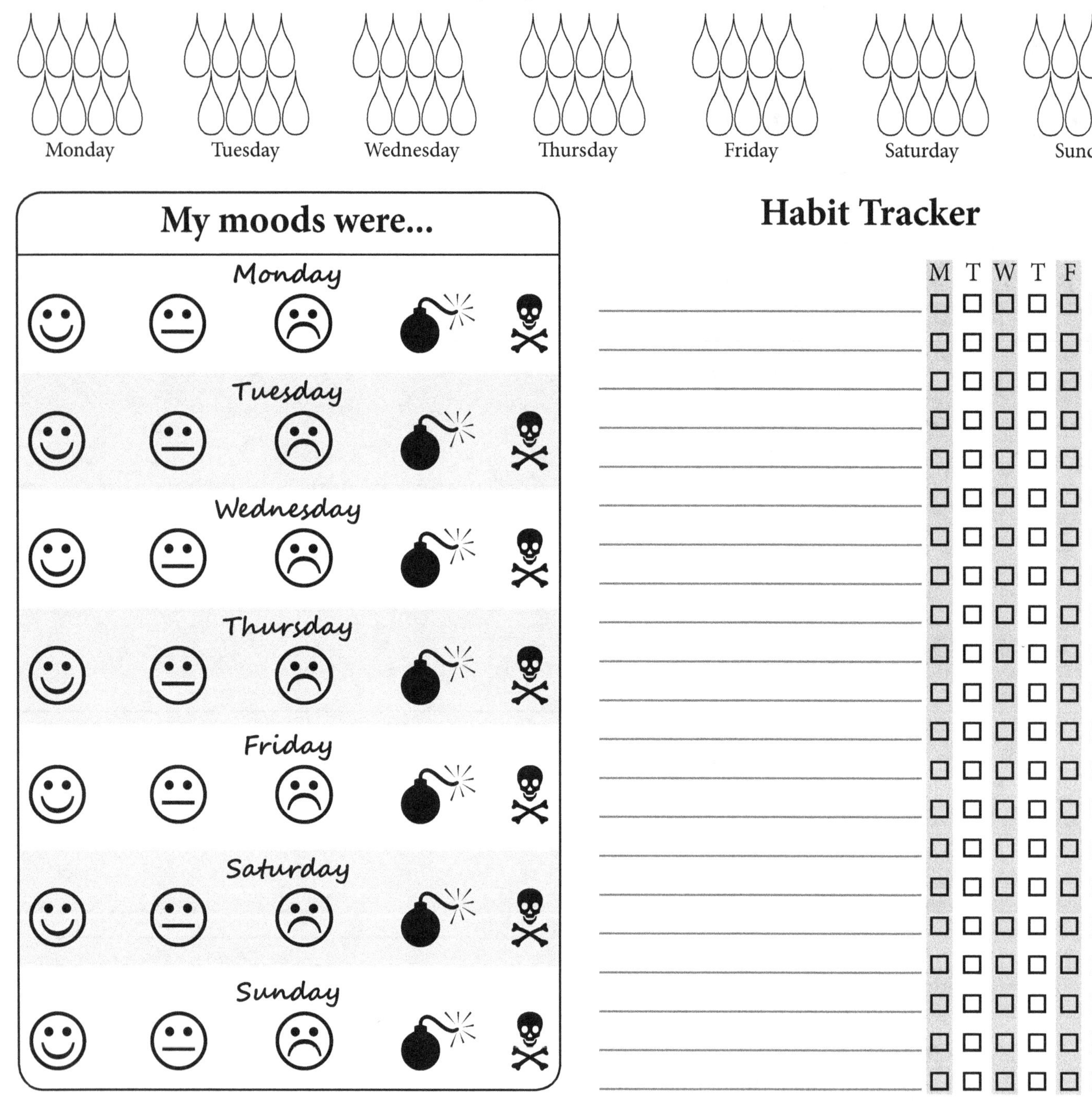

My moods were...

Monday

Tuesday

Wednesday

Thursday

Friday

Saturday

Sunday

Habit Tracker

M T W T F S S

Inspirations ❁ Affirmations ❁ Gratitudes

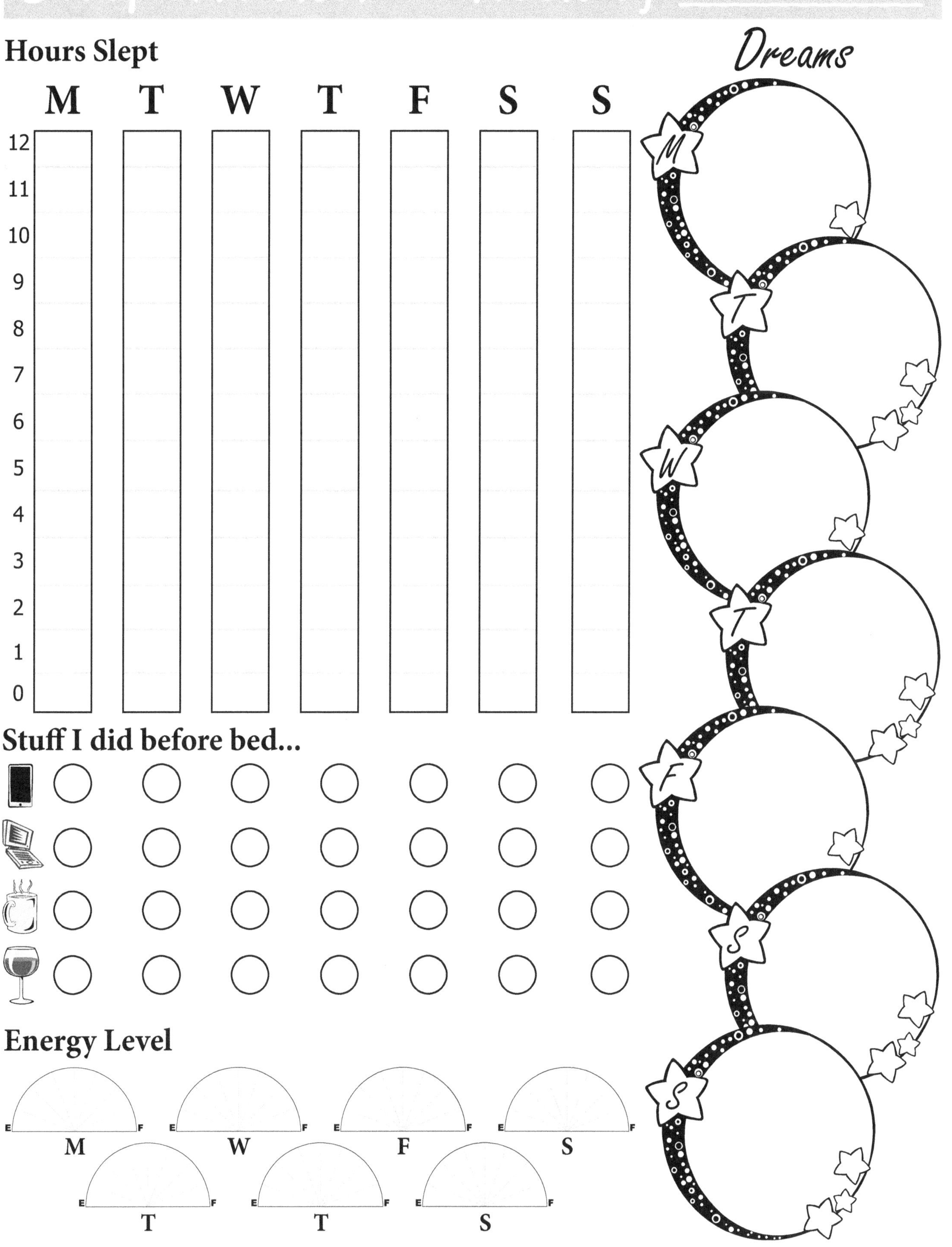

Sleep Tracker ❀ Week of __________
Hours Slept
Dreams
M T W T F S S
12
11
10
9
8
7
6
5
4
3
2
1
0
Stuff I did before bed...
Energy Level
M
T
W
T
F
S
S
M
T
W
T
F
S
E F
E F
E F
E F
E F
E F
E F

Exercise Tracker

Type of Exercise	Amount	Notes	M	T	W	T	F	S	S
			☐	☐	☐	☐	☐	☐	☐
			☐	☐	☐	☐	☐	☐	☐
			☐	☐	☐	☐	☐	☐	☐
			☐	☐	☐	☐	☐	☐	☐
			☐	☐	☐	☐	☐	☐	☐
			☐	☐	☐	☐	☐	☐	☐
			☐	☐	☐	☐	☐	☐	☐
			☐	☐	☐	☐	☐	☐	☐
			☐	☐	☐	☐	☐	☐	☐
			☐	☐	☐	☐	☐	☐	☐

Food Tracker

Monday

Breakfast	
Lunch	
Dinner	
Snacks	

Tuesday

Breakfast	
Lunch	
Dinner	
Snacks	

Wednesday

Breakfast	
Lunch	
Dinner	
Snacks	

Thursday

Breakfast	
Lunch	
Dinner	
Snacks	

Friday

Breakfast	
Lunch	
Dinner	
Snacks	

Saturday

Breakfast	
Lunch	
Dinner	
Snacks	

Sunday

Breakfast	
Lunch	
Dinner	
Snacks	

Date: ______________________________

Neck: ______________________________

Chest: ______________________________

Left Arm: ______________________________

Right Arm: ______________________________

Waist: ______________________________

Hips: ______________________________

Left Thigh: ______________________________

Right Thigh: ______________________________

Left Calf: ______________________________

Right Calf: ______________________________

Weekly Weigh-In

Weight: ______________________________

I drank this much water: (each droplet represents 8 oz./227 ml)

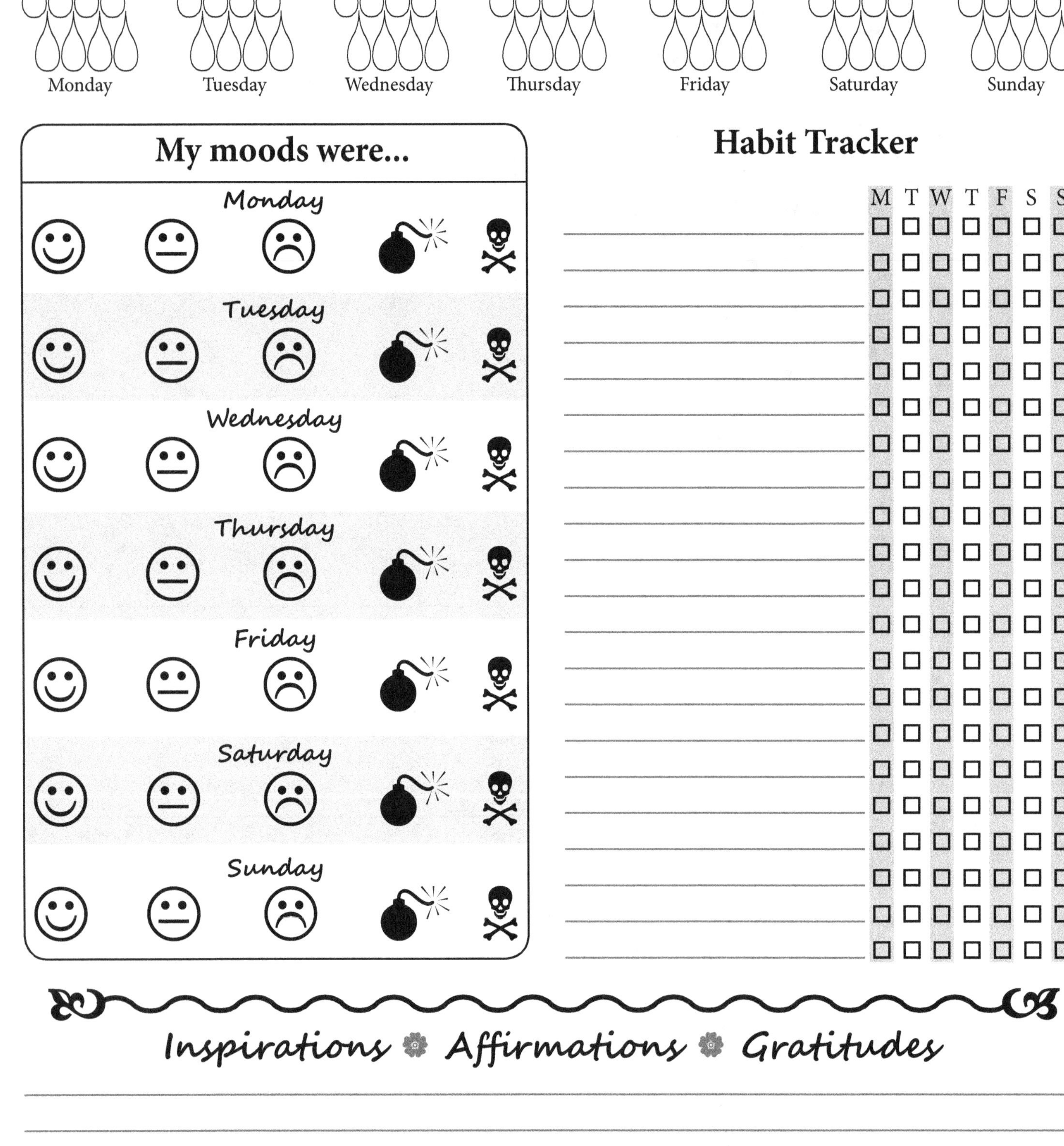

Inspirations ❀ Affirmations ❀ Gratitudes

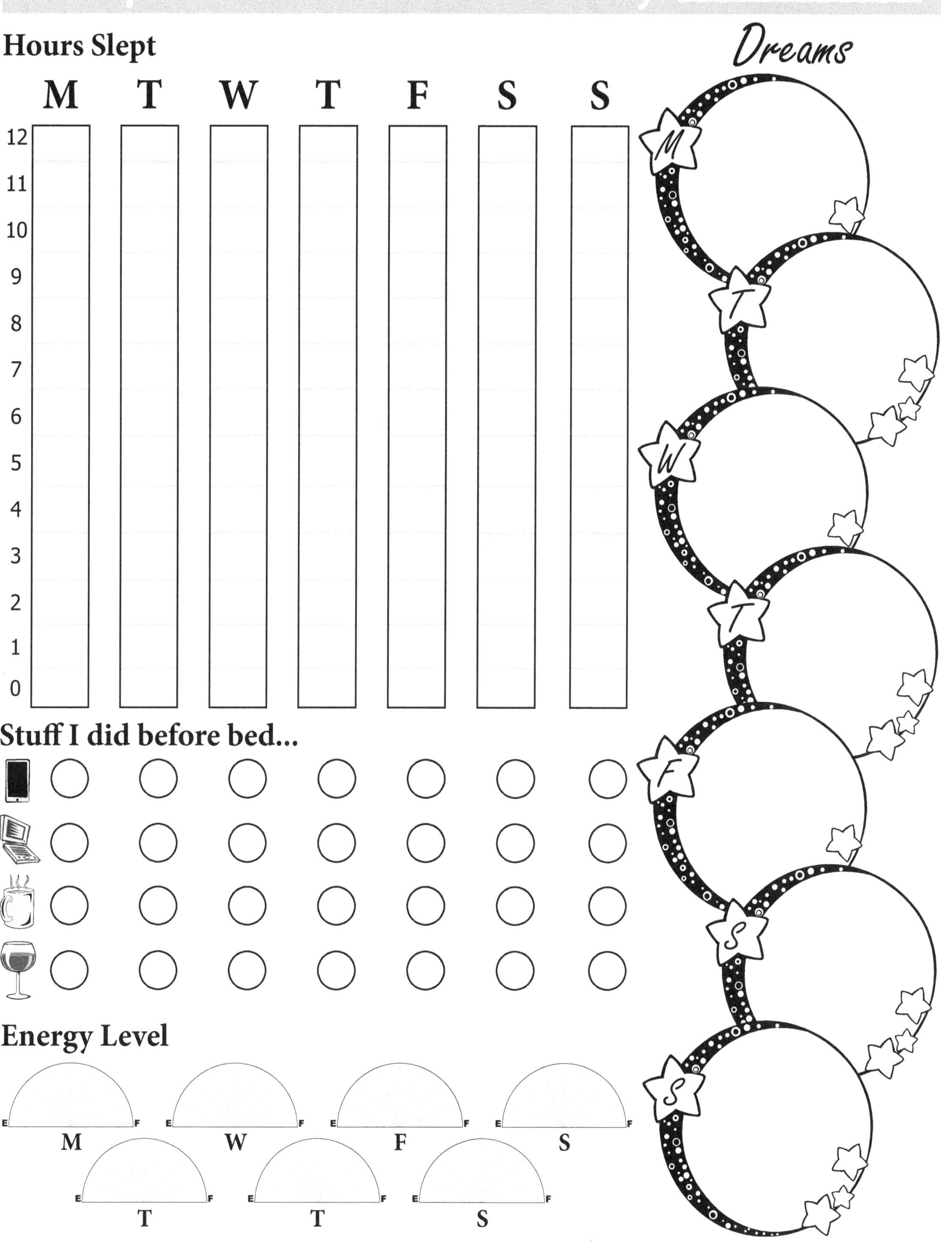

Sleep Tracker ❀ Week of ______
Hours Slept
M T W T F S S
Dreams
12
11
10
9
8
7
6
5
4
3
2
1
0
Stuff I did before bed...
Energy Level
E F
M
E F
T
E F
W
E F
T
E F
F
E F
S
E F
S
M
T
W
T
F
S
S

Exercise Tracker

Type of Exercise	Amount	Notes	M	T	W	T	F	S	S
			☐	☐	☐	☐	☐	☐	☐
			☐	☐	☐	☐	☐	☐	☐
			☐	☐	☐	☐	☐	☐	☐
			☐	☐	☐	☐	☐	☐	☐
			☐	☐	☐	☐	☐	☐	☐
			☐	☐	☐	☐	☐	☐	☐
			☐	☐	☐	☐	☐	☐	☐
			☐	☐	☐	☐	☐	☐	☐
			☐	☐	☐	☐	☐	☐	☐
			☐	☐	☐	☐	☐	☐	☐

Food Tracker

Monday

Breakfast	
Lunch	
Dinner	
Snacks	

Tuesday

Breakfast	
Lunch	
Dinner	
Snacks	

Wednesday

Breakfast	
Lunch	
Dinner	
Snacks	

Thursday

Breakfast	
Lunch	
Dinner	
Snacks	

Friday

Breakfast	
Lunch	
Dinner	
Snacks	

Saturday

Breakfast	
Lunch	
Dinner	
Snacks	

Sunday

Breakfast	
Lunch	
Dinner	
Snacks	

Date: _______________________________________

Neck: _______________________________________

Chest: _______________________________________

Left Arm: _______________________________________

Right Arm: _______________________________________

Waist: _______________________________________

Hips: _______________________________________

Left Thigh: _______________________________________

Right Thigh: _______________________________________

Left Calf: _______________________________________

Right Calf: _______________________________________

Weekly Weigh-In

Weight: _______________________________________

I drank this much water: (each droplet represents 8 oz./227 ml)

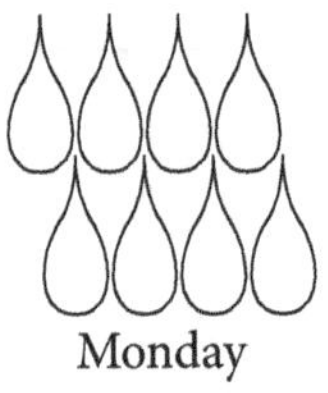
Monday

Tuesday

Wednesday

Thursday

Friday

Saturday

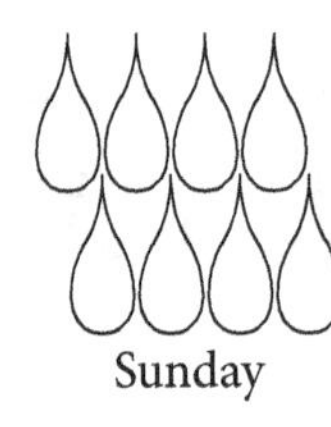
Sunday

My moods were...

Monday

Tuesday

Wednesday

Thursday

Friday

Saturday

Sunday

Habit Tracker

Inspirations ❁ Affirmations ❁ Gratitudes

Hours Slept

	M	T	W	T	F	S	S

12
11
10
9
8
7
6
5
4
3
2
1
0

Dreams

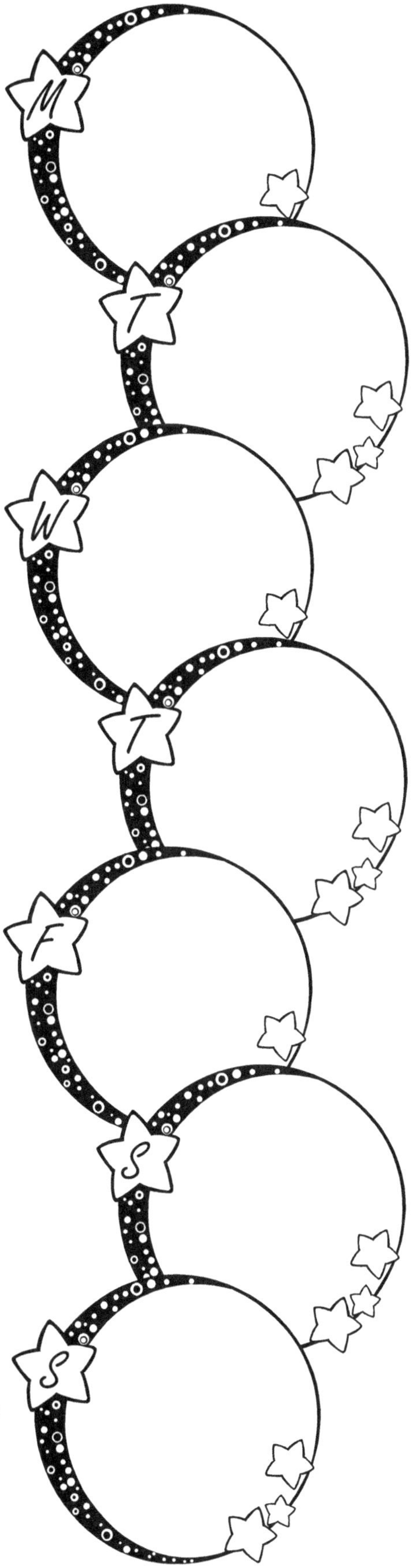

M
T
W
T
F
S
S

Stuff I did before bed...

Energy Level

M T W T F S S

E ... F

Exercise Tracker

Type of Exercise	Amount	Notes	M	T	W	T	F	S	S
			☐	☐	☐	☐	☐	☐	☐
			☐	☐	☐	☐	☐	☐	☐
			☐	☐	☐	☐	☐	☐	☐
			☐	☐	☐	☐	☐	☐	☐
			☐	☐	☐	☐	☐	☐	☐
			☐	☐	☐	☐	☐	☐	☐
			☐	☐	☐	☐	☐	☐	☐
			☐	☐	☐	☐	☐	☐	☐
			☐	☐	☐	☐	☐	☐	☐
			☐	☐	☐	☐	☐	☐	☐

Food Tracker

Monday

Breakfast	
Lunch	
Dinner	
Snacks	

Tuesday

Breakfast	
Lunch	
Dinner	
Snacks	

Wednesday

Breakfast	
Lunch	
Dinner	
Snacks	

Thursday

Breakfast	
Lunch	
Dinner	
Snacks	

Friday

Breakfast	
Lunch	
Dinner	
Snacks	

Saturday

Breakfast	
Lunch	
Dinner	
Snacks	

Sunday

Breakfast	
Lunch	
Dinner	
Snacks	

Date: ______________________________

Neck: ______________________________

Chest: ______________________________

Left Arm: ______________________________

Right Arm: ______________________________

Waist: ______________________________

Hips: ______________________________

Left Thigh: ______________________________

Right Thigh: ______________________________

Left Calf: ______________________________

Right Calf: ______________________________

Weekly Weigh-In

Weight: ______________________________

I drank this much water: (each droplet represents 8 oz./227 ml)

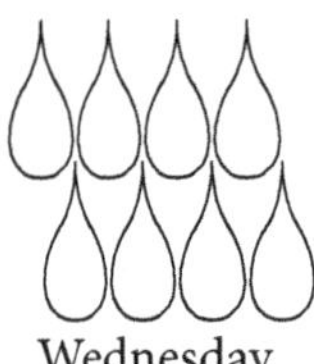
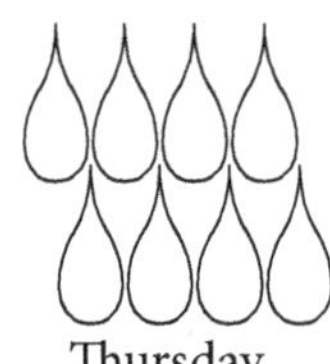

Monday	Tuesday	Wednesday	Thursday	Friday	Saturday	Sunday

My moods were...

Monday

Tuesday

Wednesday

Thursday

Friday

Saturday

Sunday

Habit Tracker

M	T	W	T	F	S	S
☐	☐	☐	☐	☐	☐	☐
☐	☐	☐	☐	☐	☐	☐
☐	☐	☐	☐	☐	☐	☐
☐	☐	☐	☐	☐	☐	☐
☐	☐	☐	☐	☐	☐	☐
☐	☐	☐	☐	☐	☐	☐
☐	☐	☐	☐	☐	☐	☐
☐	☐	☐	☐	☐	☐	☐
☐	☐	☐	☐	☐	☐	☐
☐	☐	☐	☐	☐	☐	☐
☐	☐	☐	☐	☐	☐	☐
☐	☐	☐	☐	☐	☐	☐
☐	☐	☐	☐	☐	☐	☐
☐	☐	☐	☐	☐	☐	☐
☐	☐	☐	☐	☐	☐	☐
☐	☐	☐	☐	☐	☐	☐
☐	☐	☐	☐	☐	☐	☐
☐	☐	☐	☐	☐	☐	☐

Inspirations ❀ Affirmations ❀ Gratitudes

Sleep Tracker ✿ Week of _______

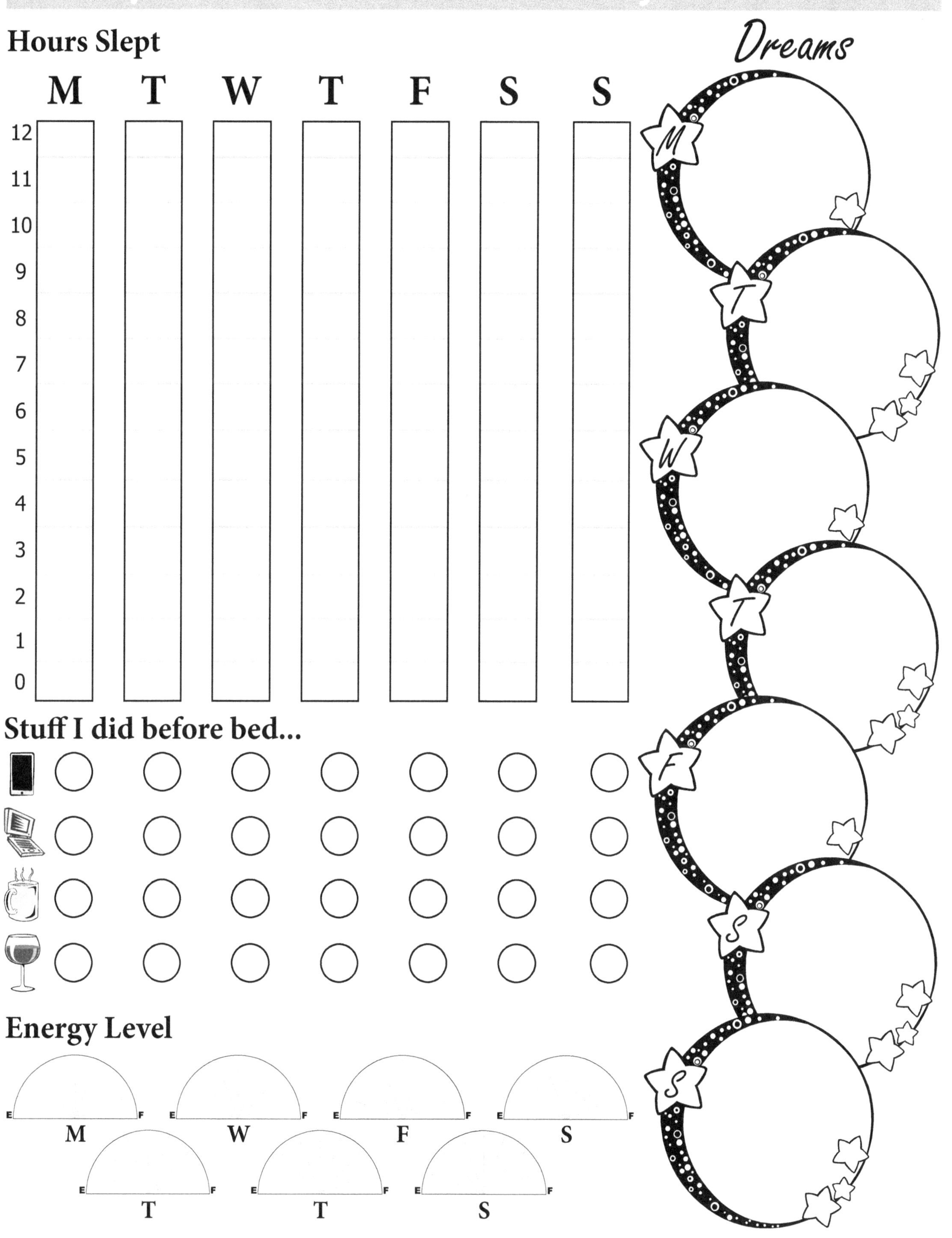

The week of: _______________

Exercise Tracker

Type of Exercise	Amount	Notes	M	T	W	T	F	S	S
			☐	☐	☐	☐	☐	☐	☐
			☐	☐	☐	☐	☐	☐	☐
			☐	☐	☐	☐	☐	☐	☐
			☐	☐	☐	☐	☐	☐	☐
			☐	☐	☐	☐	☐	☐	☐
			☐	☐	☐	☐	☐	☐	☐
			☐	☐	☐	☐	☐	☐	☐
			☐	☐	☐	☐	☐	☐	☐
			☐	☐	☐	☐	☐	☐	☐
			☐	☐	☐	☐	☐	☐	☐

Food Tracker

Monday

Breakfast	
Lunch	
Dinner	
Snacks	

Tuesday

Breakfast	
Lunch	
Dinner	
Snacks	

Wednesday

Breakfast	
Lunch	
Dinner	
Snacks	

Thursday

Breakfast	
Lunch	
Dinner	
Snacks	

Friday

Breakfast	
Lunch	
Dinner	
Snacks	

Saturday

Breakfast	
Lunch	
Dinner	
Snacks	

Sunday

Breakfast	
Lunch	
Dinner	
Snacks	

Date: ______________________________

Neck: ______________________________

Chest: ______________________________

Left Arm: ______________________________

Right Arm: ______________________________

Waist: ______________________________

Hips: ______________________________

Left Thigh: ______________________________

Right Thigh: ______________________________

Left Calf: ______________________________

Right Calf: ______________________________

Weekly Weigh-In

Weight: ______________________________

The week of: ____________

I drank this much water: (each droplet represents 8 oz./227 ml)

Monday Tuesday Wednesday Thursday Friday Saturday Sunday

My moods were...

Monday

Tuesday

Wednesday

Thursday

Friday

Saturday

Sunday

Habit Tracker

	M	T	W	T	F	S	S
	☐	☐	☐	☐	☐	☐	☐

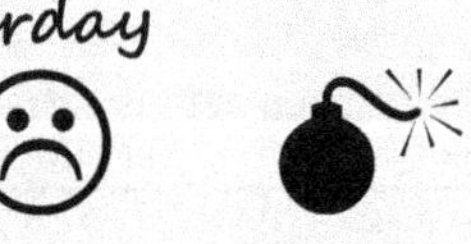

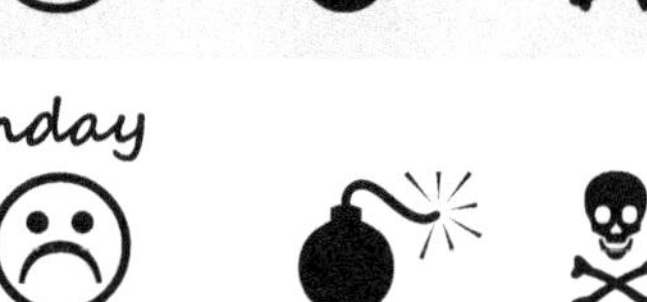

Inspirations ❁ Affirmations ❁ Gratitudes

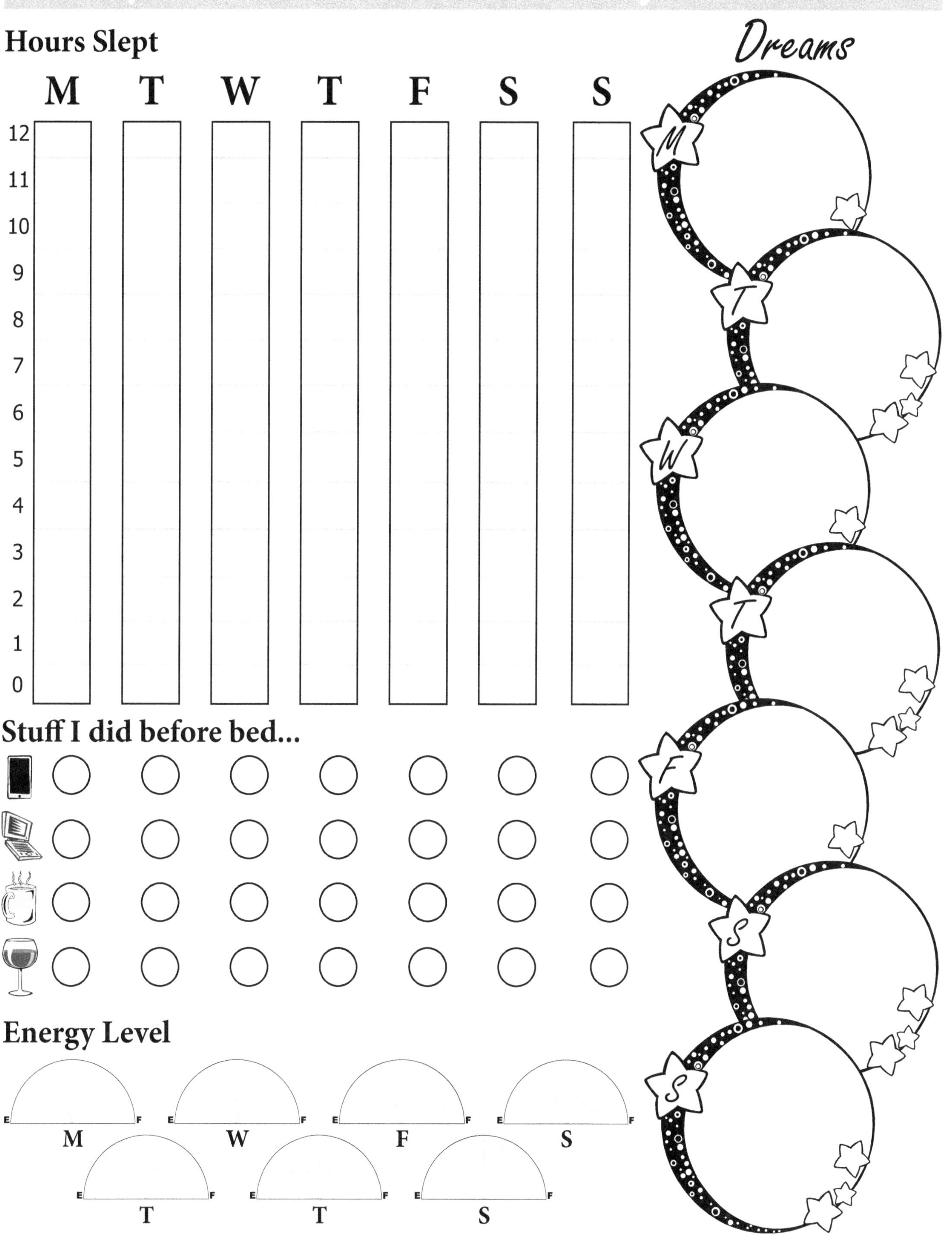

Sleep Tracker ❀ Week of ____________
Dreams
Hours Slept
M T W T F S S
12
11
10
9
8
7
6
5
4
3
2
1
0
Stuff I did before bed...
Energy Level
E F
M
E F
W
E F
F
E F
S
E F
T
E F
T
E F
S
M
T
W
T
F
S
S

The week of: _______________

Exercise Tracker

Type of Exercise	Amount	Notes	M	T	W	T	F	S	S
			☐	☐	☐	☐	☐	☐	☐
			☐	☐	☐	☐	☐	☐	☐
			☐	☐	☐	☐	☐	☐	☐
			☐	☐	☐	☐	☐	☐	☐
			☐	☐	☐	☐	☐	☐	☐
			☐	☐	☐	☐	☐	☐	☐
			☐	☐	☐	☐	☐	☐	☐
			☐	☐	☐	☐	☐	☐	☐
			☐	☐	☐	☐	☐	☐	☐
			☐	☐	☐	☐	☐	☐	☐

Food Tracker

Monday

Breakfast	
Lunch	
Dinner	
Snacks	

Tuesday

Breakfast	
Lunch	
Dinner	
Snacks	

Wednesday

Breakfast	
Lunch	
Dinner	
Snacks	

Thursday

Breakfast	
Lunch	
Dinner	
Snacks	

Friday

Breakfast	
Lunch	
Dinner	
Snacks	

Saturday

Breakfast	
Lunch	
Dinner	
Snacks	

Sunday

Breakfast	
Lunch	
Dinner	
Snacks	

Date: _______________________________

Neck: _______________________________

Chest: _______________________________

Left Arm: _______________________________

Right Arm: _______________________________

Waist: _______________________________

Hips: _______________________________

Left Thigh: _______________________________

Right Thigh: _______________________________

Left Calf: _______________________________

Right Calf: _______________________________

Weekly Weigh-In

Weight: _______________________________

I drank this much water: (each droplet represents 8 oz./227 ml)

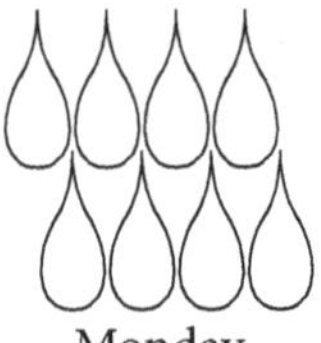
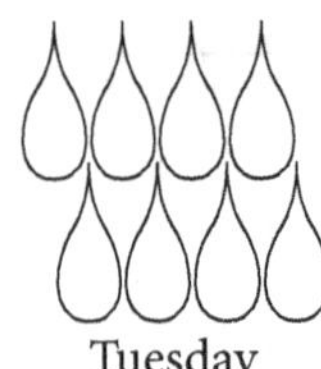
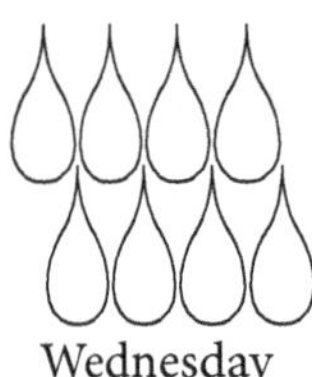
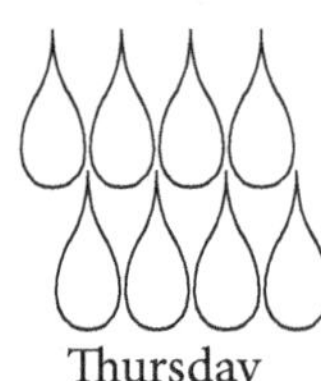

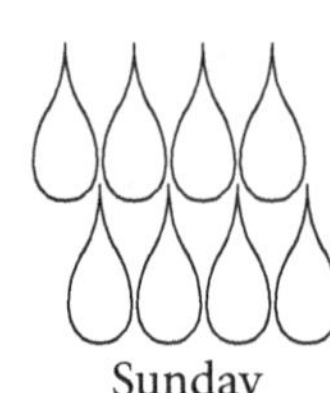

Monday   Tuesday   Wednesday   Thursday   Friday   Saturday   Sunday

My moods were...

Monday

Tuesday

Wednesday

Thursday

Friday

Saturday

Sunday

Habit Tracker

	M	T	W	T	F	S	S
__________	☐	☐	☐	☐	☐	☐	☐
__________	☐	☐	☐	☐	☐	☐	☐
__________	☐	☐	☐	☐	☐	☐	☐
__________	☐	☐	☐	☐	☐	☐	☐
__________	☐	☐	☐	☐	☐	☐	☐
__________	☐	☐	☐	☐	☐	☐	☐
__________	☐	☐	☐	☐	☐	☐	☐
__________	☐	☐	☐	☐	☐	☐	☐
__________	☐	☐	☐	☐	☐	☐	☐
__________	☐	☐	☐	☐	☐	☐	☐
__________	☐	☐	☐	☐	☐	☐	☐
__________	☐	☐	☐	☐	☐	☐	☐
__________	☐	☐	☐	☐	☐	☐	☐
__________	☐	☐	☐	☐	☐	☐	☐
__________	☐	☐	☐	☐	☐	☐	☐
__________	☐	☐	☐	☐	☐	☐	☐
__________	☐	☐	☐	☐	☐	☐	☐
__________	☐	☐	☐	☐	☐	☐	☐

Inspirations ❀ Affirmations ❀ Gratitudes

____

____

____

____

____

Sleep Tracker ✿ Week of _______

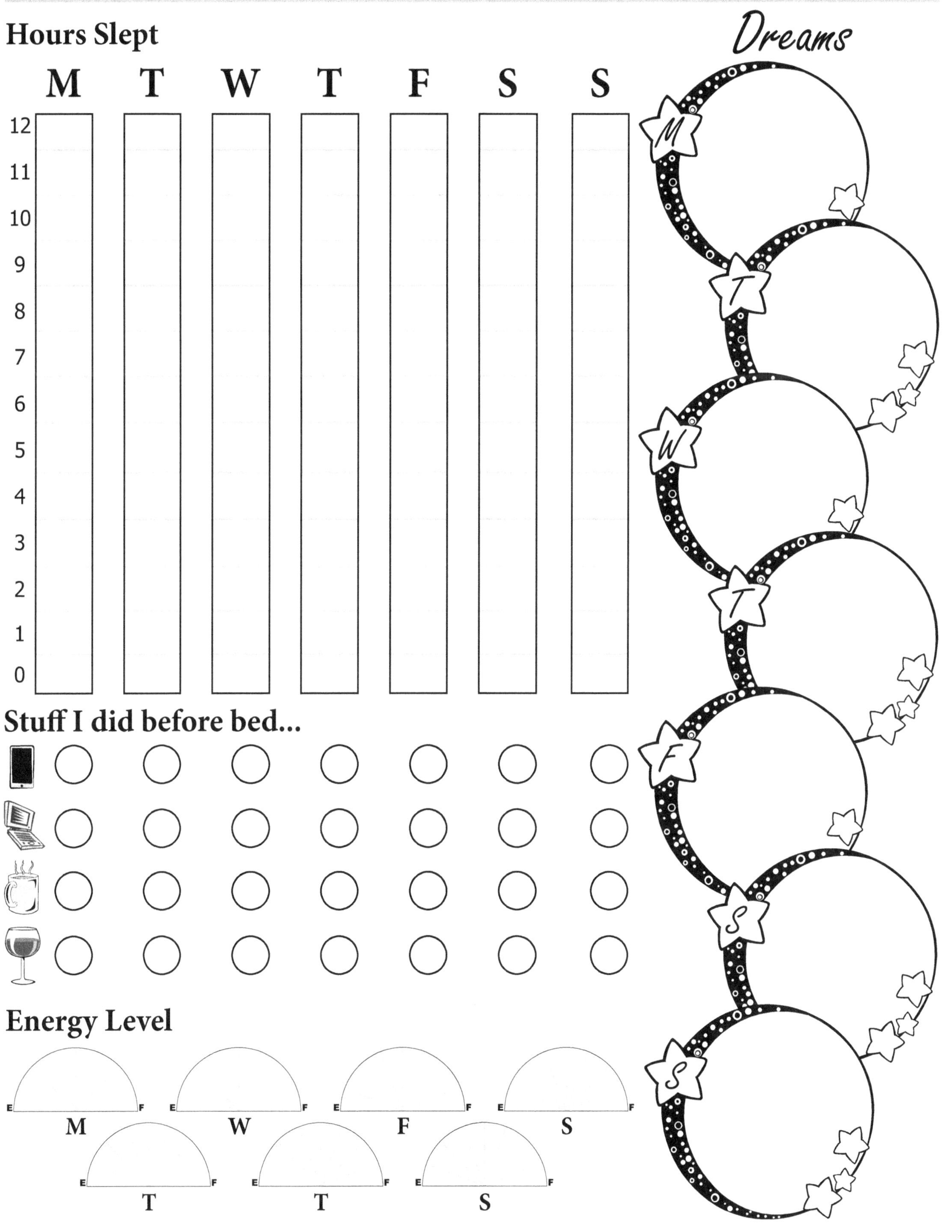

The week of: _______________

Exercise Tracker

Type of Exercise	Amount	Notes	M	T	W	T	F	S	S
			☐	☐	☐	☐	☐	☐	☐
			☐	☐	☐	☐	☐	☐	☐
			☐	☐	☐	☐	☐	☐	☐
			☐	☐	☐	☐	☐	☐	☐
			☐	☐	☐	☐	☐	☐	☐
			☐	☐	☐	☐	☐	☐	☐
			☐	☐	☐	☐	☐	☐	☐
			☐	☐	☐	☐	☐	☐	☐
			☐	☐	☐	☐	☐	☐	☐
			☐	☐	☐	☐	☐	☐	☐

Food Tracker

Monday

Breakfast	
Lunch	
Dinner	
Snacks	

Tuesday

Breakfast	
Lunch	
Dinner	
Snacks	

Wednesday

Breakfast	
Lunch	
Dinner	
Snacks	

Thursday

Breakfast	
Lunch	
Dinner	
Snacks	

Friday

Breakfast	
Lunch	
Dinner	
Snacks	

Saturday

Breakfast	
Lunch	
Dinner	
Snacks	

Sunday

Breakfast	
Lunch	
Dinner	
Snacks	

Date: _______________________

Neck: _______________________

Chest: _______________________

Left Arm: _______________________

Right Arm: _______________________

Waist: _______________________

Hips: _______________________

Left Thigh: _______________________

Right Thigh: _______________________

Left Calf: _______________________

Right Calf: _______________________

Weekly Weigh-In

Weight: _______________________

I drank this much water: (each droplet represents 8 oz./227 ml)

Monday Tuesday Wednesday Thursday Friday Saturday Sunday

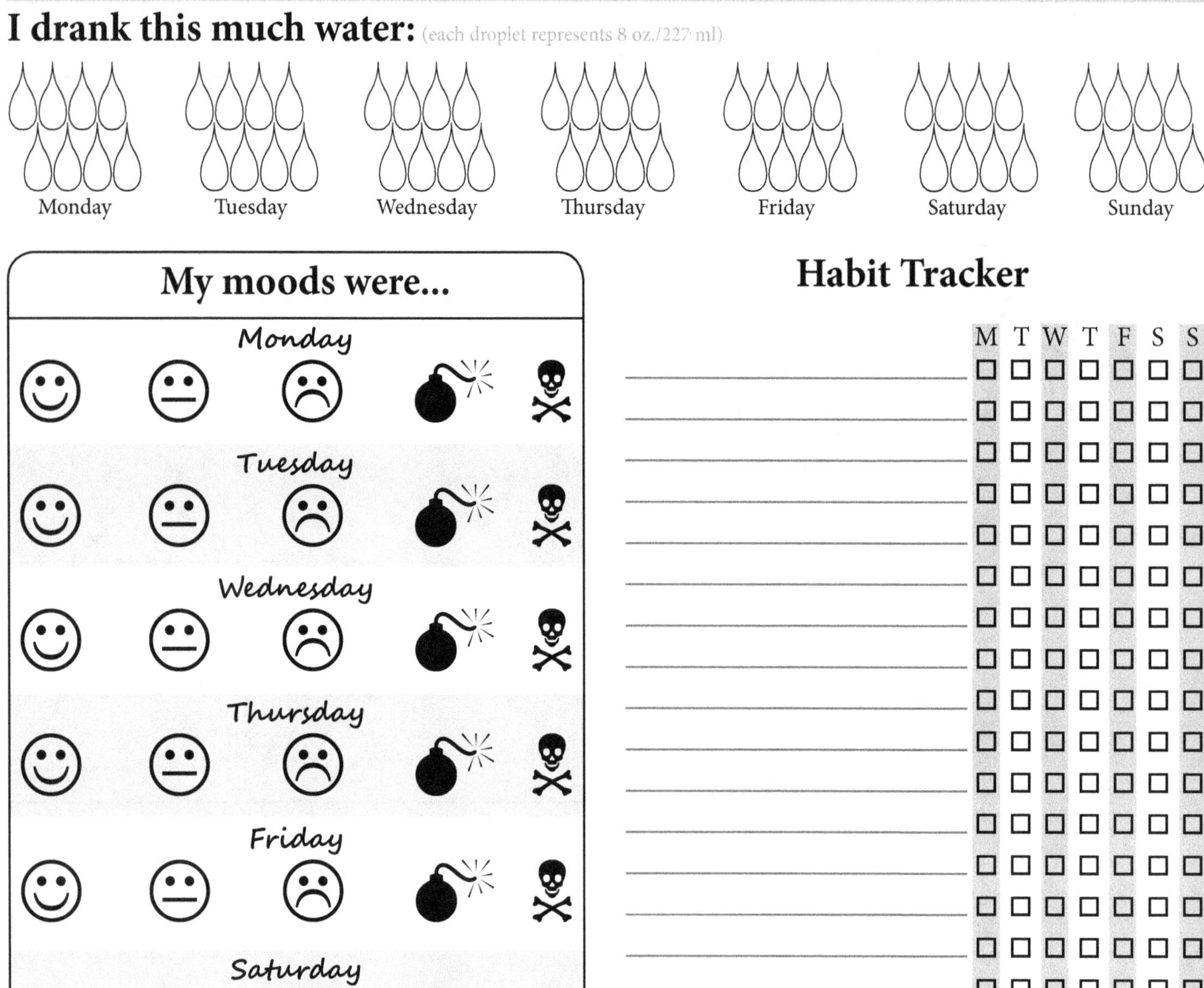

My moods were...

Monday

Tuesday

Wednesday

Thursday

Friday

Saturday

Sunday

Habit Tracker

M T W T F S S

Inspirations ❀ Affirmations ❀ Gratitudes

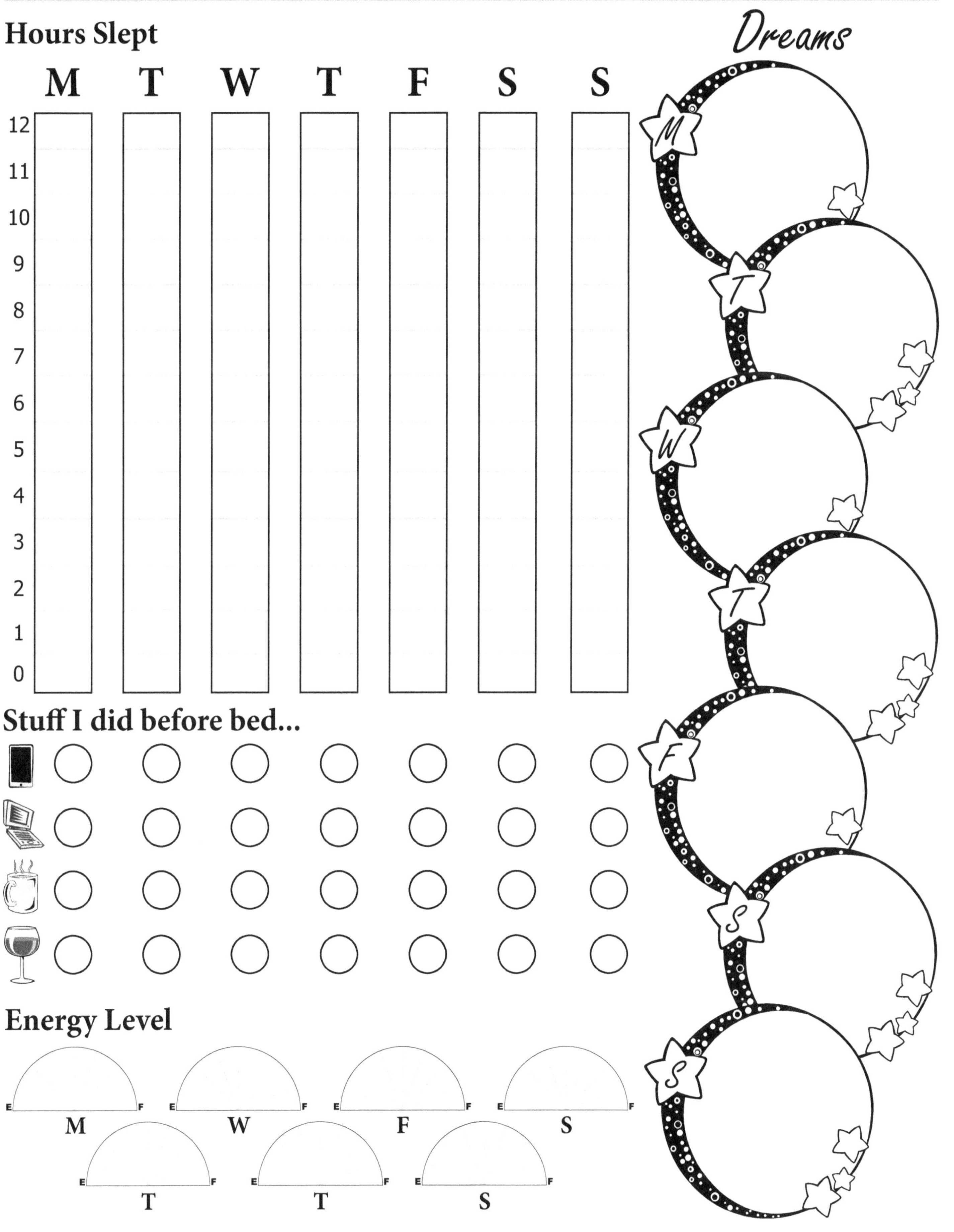

Sleep Tracker ❀ Week of _______
Dreams
Hours Slept
M T W T F S S
12
11
10
9
8
7
6
5
4
3
2
1
0
Stuff I did before bed...
Energy Level
E F
M
E F
T
E F
W
E F
T
E F
F
E F
S
E F
S
M
T
W
T
F
S
S

The week of: _______________________

Exercise Tracker

Type of Exercise	Amount	Notes	M	T	W	T	F	S	S
			☐	☐	☐	☐	☐	☐	☐
			☐	☐	☐	☐	☐	☐	☐
			☐	☐	☐	☐	☐	☐	☐
			☐	☐	☐	☐	☐	☐	☐
			☐	☐	☐	☐	☐	☐	☐
			☐	☐	☐	☐	☐	☐	☐
			☐	☐	☐	☐	☐	☐	☐
			☐	☐	☐	☐	☐	☐	☐
			☐	☐	☐	☐	☐	☐	☐
			☐	☐	☐	☐	☐	☐	☐

Food Tracker

Monday

Breakfast	
Lunch	
Dinner	
Snacks	

Tuesday

Breakfast	
Lunch	
Dinner	
Snacks	

Wednesday

Breakfast	
Lunch	
Dinner	
Snacks	

Thursday

Breakfast	
Lunch	
Dinner	
Snacks	

Friday

Breakfast	
Lunch	
Dinner	
Snacks	

Saturday

Breakfast	
Lunch	
Dinner	
Snacks	

Sunday

Breakfast	
Lunch	
Dinner	
Snacks	

Date: _______________________________

Neck: _________________________________

Chest: ________________________________

Left Arm: _____________________________

Right Arm: ____________________________

Waist: ________________________________

Hips: _________________________________

Left Thigh: ___________________________

Right Thigh: __________________________

Left Calf: ____________________________

Right Calf: ___________________________

Weekly Weigh-In

Weight: _______________________________

6-Month Period Tracker

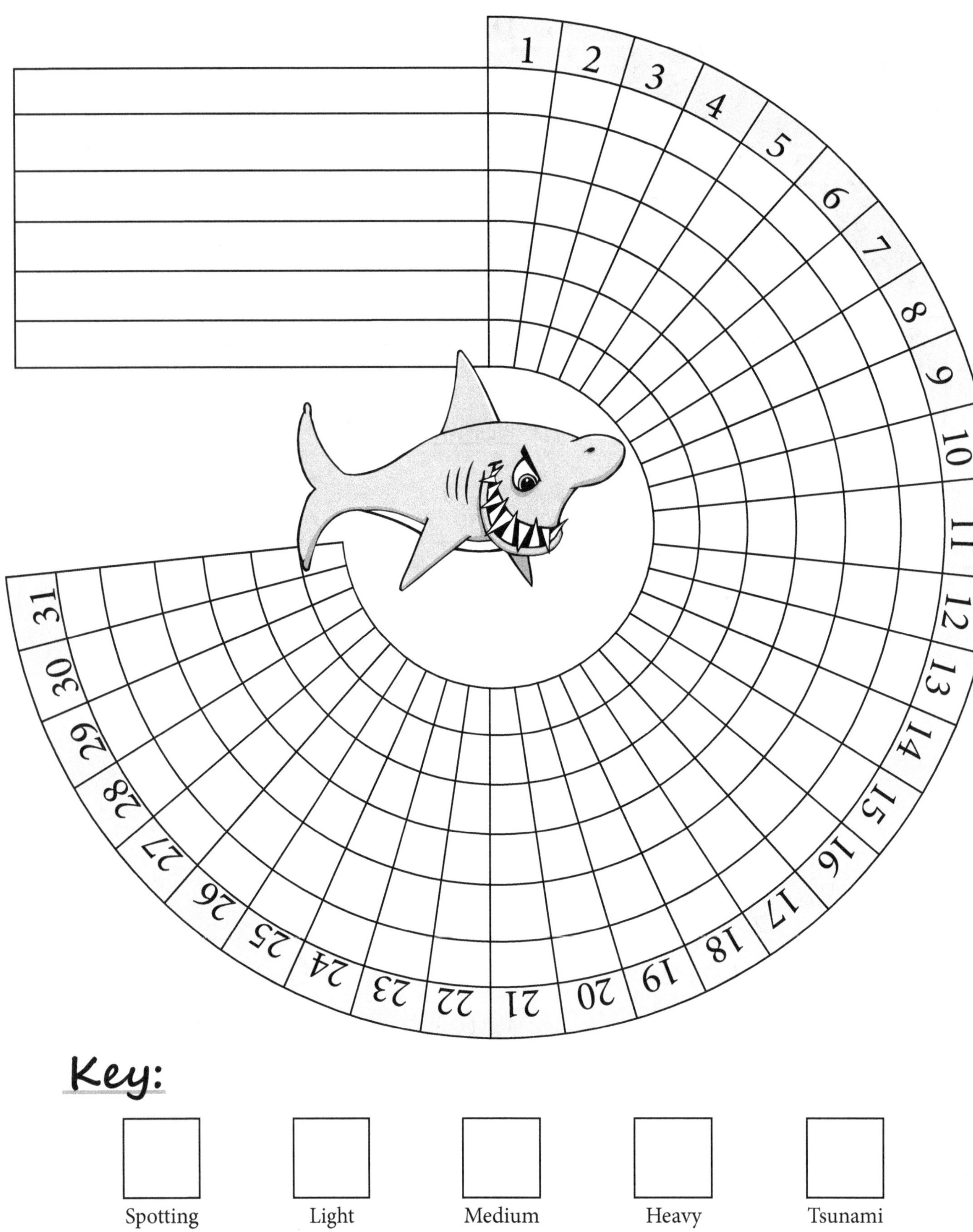

Key:

Spotting   Light   Medium   Heavy   Tsunami

My 6-Month Weight Loss Journey

Weight:	Week: 1	2	3	4	5	6	7	8	9	10	11	12	13	14	15	16	17	18	19	20	21	22	23	24	25	26

1 MONTH GOAL

3 MONTH GOAL

6 MONTH GOAL

1 Month Reward

3 Month Reward

6 Month Reward

YAY!

You made it to the end. Congratulations.

Now you know so much more about yourself than ever before — like how much you sleep, how much water you drink, what you dream about — and you've been working on making the important things in your life into *HABITS*.

Don't worry if some of those habits (all of them?) are not quite "there" yet — it's a process.☺

Feel free to use this *My Crazy Life* tracker as a kind of road map to the life you want, and if there's anything missing from it that would have made it perfect, please let me know.

I might just add it in there!

**Thanks so much for making me a part of your journey,
and I'll see you next time.** ♥